The Great Escape
The Successful Woman's Guide to Escaping the 9-5

Amy Mewborn, CFP

appropriate business advisors and discuss your personal situation with them before any decisions are made in your business!

The Great Escape: The Successful Woman's Guide to Escaping the 9-5

Business and Money - Small Business and Entrepreneurship –
New Business Enterprises
ISBN-10: 0692706984
ISBN-13: 978-0692706985

Dedicated to:

- My husband, Mike
- My mastermind girls and the women business owners in my life who are always pushing me for more!
- My parents, Danny and Lisa

Mike, you have supported me in just about anything I have ever wanted to do. I never could have known that night on the beach in Hawaii what a great friend, partner, and supporter you would be. I thank God every day (well almost every day) for you and your love! ;-)

Mom and Dad, you have both made so many sacrifices for everything we ever had. From early in my life, you have always pushed me to work hard and achieve more. You also always made me feel like anything was possible with hard work and faith in God. I never could have done the things in my life that I have without you guys in my corner. Your love and sacrifices have not gone unnoticed – even if they weren't appreciated so much in those teen years! I love you both!

Introduction:

Growing up, I was always told to work hard and get a good job, work there for years, save for retirement, and hopefully also have a pension! Oh, if jobs only still provided pensions and security. Today, people rarely stay in the same job more than a few years. And there is no such thing as job security. And a pension – yeah right! I left a fifteen-year finance career in the middle of my prime earning years to start my own business.

I did it for two reasons:

1. My job was actually cutting salaries and benefits due to the economy.
2. After years advising multi-million dollar families and corporations, it became very clear, the people with true wealth were the business owners, not the employees!

In over 20 years in business, I have helped multi-million-dollar business owners, multi-million dollar businesses, and fledgling entrepreneurs. And what I found is that to truly be able to make business decisions from a position of strength, you have to understand where you are, where you want to go, and how to get there.

This book is written for the woman who either wants to start a business, or wants to take their business to new heights. I will teach you the foundations of building a new business, from how to hire the best staff, hiring professionals, reading a Profit and Loss Statement, and creating balance between your business and your life! If you are putting the foundations in your business, or you are ready to scale up your business – I hope that this book can be a valuable resource to you!

If you would like access to many of the free worksheets and resources in the book – please go to **amymewborn.com/free** and get free resources to help you grow and scale your business!

Table of Contents

CHAPTER 1

You're Going to be What?

*The power of a single idea acted upon
changes lives –
Blake Mycoskie*

So you want to be an entrepreneur?

Being an entrepreneur can be a fabulous life, or it can be miserable, depending on you, your personality, your strengths, your family support, and your risk tolerance. As a serial entrepreneur and business consultant, I get a lot of questions about opening a business. I often have people reaching out to take me for coffee to "pick my brain" to determine if they have what it takes to be an entrepreneur.

Some of the biggest questions I get are:

- Should I do it?
- Is "this" a passing trend that won't be sustainable in the future?
- What if I don't make it?
- Do I have what it takes?
- How will I make the bills if this doesn't work?

I want to be VERY clear… Launching a business is NOT for the faint of heart. Launching a business takes a lot of heart and a lot of hard work. There are days when it is good, and there are days when it is bad.

Do the one thing you think you cannot do.
Fail at it. Try again. Do better the second time.
The only people who never tumble are those who
never mount the high wire. This is your moment.
Own it.
Oprah Winfrey

When I opened my first fitness studio, I didn't yet have a full staff. I taught 100% of the classes for the first two weeks. My first week, I was so tired that I actually started to pray that people wouldn't attend a class just so I could get a break. Can you imagine launching a new business and actually praying that no one would show up? That's not the ideal! But I learned within just the first week of my business opening, that it was going to take more time and energy than I had anticipated. Fortunately, I was young, I had the energy, I had the drive, and I had a super supportive spouse. But I talk to a number of business owners who after just the first week are already wondering if they made the right decision. (This is not uncommon... Most of us go through it at one point or another!)

Although I presently run two studios, my goal isn't to run two studios indefinitely. Trying to run two studios, create programs and choreography, create continuing education, consult on other studio openings, write books, coach entrepreneurs, launch programs, travel around the country speaking and educating, and still have a life – I'm a busy girl. Fortunately, I genuinely love what I do, but it is exhausting to try to keep all these balls in the air!

This past year, I have been working with someone to potentially transfer the second studio and simplify my life! My goal is to keep one studio. It is my opportunity to interact with clients. It is my opportunity to try new exercises and choreography. It is my chance to experience what other studio owners experience on a daily basis. But having a brick and mortar location, managing a staff of 12-25, and keeping hundreds of clients happy at one time has certainly taken more energy than I thought it would!

I am always amazed that there are franchisors, company founders, and business consultants that have never owned their own business. If they have never been in the same place as their client, they can study and sympathize but will never really be able to empathize or know from experience what it is like to run that business. I feel that in order to genuinely advise, they need to have experience in what they are coaching or consulting on. I also feel that if they want to really be able to grow with their clients, they have to continue to experience some of what their clients do!

For example, we have been through a number of different financial cycles since I opened my first Pilates studio in 2006.

- I started the Pilates studio out of my house and every dollar I made after the initial certification and reformers were paid off was profit! I ran it in the evening and on the weekends and it was a way to make a bit of extra money, as well as, do something that I really enjoyed. However, after I decided I was too busy to manage my full-time job and a part-time Pilates studio, I decided to shut down the studio.
- I grew in my corporate job and made amazing money the last few years in corporate America, but I just wasn't enjoying my life anymore!

- I then opened my first fitness studio. I was working my TAIL off! After only three months in business, it was paying for itself. I kept reinvesting the profits and used that as the capital to build my second studio.
- After running the second studio, I was again making excellent money, but I was missing the business elements of corporate America!
- A few years later, I decided I wanted to train instructors and help potential studio owners open their own studios. I took my focus off of the studios to create HUGE programs. The income of the studios went down – by a lot!
- Last year I launched my training programs, and they had a year of almost $100,000 in revenue, but at the same time, I was increasing staff and expenses in the studio and hired someone else to run one of the studios start to finish. I had a year of tremendous business change and personal growth, but everything took more than I had anticipated. With all of the changes introduced in such a short period of time, this was the first year that I felt like I had genuinely bitten off more than I could chew. Fortunately, my training business and my husband's business gave us the freedom to do a ton of traveling and gave us a work life balance that I wouldn't have been able to achieve with the studios!

I'm only rich because I know when I'm wrong... I basically have survived by recognizing my mistakes.
George Soros

So, guess what? It was time to re-evaluate what my goals and objectives were. I realized that I was working too hard. So, I decided to make some serious changes.

Mike and I sold the assets of the first studio. I hired a full-time manager for the second studio, and I have focused my time on the consulting side of my business. I don't know that this will be my long-term goal, but my message is this:

If something isn't working in your life – PIVOT. If you have been climbing up a certain ladder and realize it's not where you want to be, climb down (or better yet – jump) and start up another ladder. The estimation is that the average person will have seven careers in their life. The way I see it, I'm on my third career at age 40! I have not been afraid to make changes as I have gone along!

Before we get started on identifying your specific goals, let's identify a few characteristics of you and what your life would be like as an entrepreneur.

I swear that every time I started a new job in corporate America, I had to do a new personality test. Some measured my operating system, some measured my communication style. Some measured my strengths and weaknesses. Some measured my aptitude toward certain tasks. Although they all told me something about myself, it was often exhausting to get all these labels.

If you are serious about being an entrepreneur, here are some of the things I want to know.

A journey of a thousand miles
must begin with a single step...
Lao Tzu

How do you make decisions?

1. I don't need a lot of data. I trust my gut and jump in head first.
2. I want a general outline of the Problem and Solution.
3. I need to take the time to create a checklist.
4. I need all the information possible. I will create a pro/con checklist and want to consider all the "what ifs" I can imagine before any decisions are made.

If you were to put together a bike, what procedure would you follow?

1. Directions? What directions? I would open up the box and start putting it together.
2. I would look it all over, trust that it's all there and start following the directions.
3. I would put the pieces into piles to make sure that everything is there and start following the directions, and I'd go to town.
4. I would read the instructions from start to finish and ensure that all the pieces are in place before I start putting it together.

The most successful entrepreneurs are known to be quick, effective decision makers who follow their instincts. If you are someone who can't make decisions, you may find that being an entrepreneur may be harder for you than many!

The only place where success comes before work is in the dictionary.
Vidal Sassoon

Entrepreneurs Who Will Often Struggle:

- Someone Who Makes Slow Decisions
- Analysis paralysis
- Operates from fear
- Often has a scarcity mentality

Super Successful Entrepreneurs:

- Someone Who Makes Fast, Informed Decisions
- They get the facts
- They are confident in their gut
- They believe in abundance

Let your gut guide you. I'm not saying don't research and don't make an informed decision. I'm just saying, don't second guess yourself, and don't get stuck in analysis paralysis – making no decision. Indecision is actually a decision in itself!

Practical Application

In all my life I had NEVER not passed an exam. I took some of the hardest exams in the country – including the financial planning exams for my Series 7 license, the exam for my Series 24, and my two-day Certified Financial Planner exam. However, when I moved to California, I went to sit for the insurance exam. I had already passed the insurance exam in Indiana. At the time, passing was 80%. I figured I could do that in my sleep, so I didn't really study for it at all. It was only something like a two-hour exam. I felt not only confident, but cocky!

Imagine my surprise when I was sitting there in the exam, and I just didn't know some of the answers! For the first time in my entire history of exam taking, I was finding myself second guessing my answers and using the full amount of time, but also, I found myself going back and re-reading the questions and my answers and making changes! That is NOT something I did! I genuinely believed in myself. I knew this business. I knew what I was doing. For the first time in my entire life, I was actually going and erasing my answers – which had been my initial instinct - only to instead make changes.

Guess what happened? ... I did NOT pass this exam, and I missed it by one question! I can tell you without a doubt that had I just followed my gut and not made changes to my answers, I would have passed that test. I knew what I was doing, but because it was harder than I expected it to be, I second guessed myself and didn't just follow my gut! Shoot! This wasn't a tragedy; I was able to retake the test the next month, and it only cost me a few hundred dollars, but it really hurt my pride! As a business owner, you must be willing to follow your instincts and move. If you spend too much time second guessing yourself, you'll never succeed.

Success is walking from failure to failure
with no loss of enthusiasm.
Winston Churchill

Entrepreneurs Don't:

- Make excuses
- Blame others for failures
- Sit and wait

I know a number of people who NEVER see anything as their fault. As a business owner, I can tell you – the buck stops here – literally and figuratively. If someone on my staff makes a mistake, it is my mistake too, and it is my butt and reputation on the line. Any time we have a customer service failure, I am reminded that any customer service failure is MY reputation and that I am the one that needs to figure out how to make it right. Also, I can make excuses for why something doesn't get done, but ultimately, in my business, everything stops or starts with me!

If you are sitting there making excuses for why your life isn't the way you want it to be, it is no one's fault but your own. If your goal is to be an entrepreneur, you need to be able to accept the wins as well as the losses. If you can't, then you are going to struggle as a business owner!

Practical Application
No Excuses and My Big House

Mike and I bought an amazing home in 2005. It is 3700 square feet and has room for almost anything we would want it to be. We have no kids. Mike has a "fun room" with a pool table; we have a guest "suite" with a bedroom, living room, and bathroom. We each have our own offices, and I have a fitness/video studio – all of this within our home.

People always comment on what a gorgeous home it is and how lucky we are, but what people don't know about us and this home is that sometimes it feels like the noose around my neck. You see, we bought this house when I was a full time financial planner and Mike was selling software full time. We each had steady paychecks. We knew we could make that mortgage payment.

However, less than a month into our new home, (we hadn't even made our first mortgage payment yet) Mike was laid off from his job. Oh my gosh! My mom was in town and we were out shopping, and I got the call that his company had been purchased and half the office was laid off. All of a sudden, none of the reasons mattered – I was just unsure how we'd be making the payments for long!

We immediately sat down and circled the wagons. and we decided to rent out the guest suite – which helped us bridge the gap while Mike was starting his new business as a realtor. Fortunately, as we each built our businesses, we made it all work and were able to reclaim our house and get past that tough time.

However, we found ourselves back in a challenge this past year. Mike's dad died of cancer recently. Mike spent between last May and last November flying back and forth between California and Florida to spend as much time with him as possible. It was amazing that he was self- employed and had the ability to fly back and forth, and that he had the flexibility to actually put his family first. Yet, at the same time, as a self- employed person – if you stop working, your business stops working! For six months last year, he was literally telling clients, "I just want to let you know I'm leaving in two weeks so I may not be in town to take you out looking for properties." Talk about literally shutting down his business! He didn't necessarily agree that this was what he did, but each time he said that, I felt like a part of me died inside. I felt like MY family wasn't important. I couldn't believe it as he kept sending clients away and literally was manifesting NO clients.

So let's fast forward almost a year – it took about six months to ramp up his business again. So for those six months, we kept getting further and further behind, which meant that for a FULL YEAR, we had been receiving little to no income from Mike's business to support our expensive lifestyle. During that time, I had been blaming Mike. I had been sitting here complaining to him (and about him). I had been ANGRY that we had been struggling and that I felt like he wasn't showing up for me.

You know what though – we're a team. If instead of putting that energy into being angry, blaming him, and making excuses, I had been working harder, smarter and innovating new programs, we would likely be in a different place! Fast forward a year, and Mike had the absolute best year of his entire adult life! Mike is one who lives his life with the belief that he hasn't lost until he gives up, which is hard for me. He proved that as an entrepreneur, you need to be resilient. After a bad year, you need to be able to pick yourself up, dust yourself off, and just work harder and smarter to achieve your goals. This was a lesson for me - one that I hope to remember for years to come!

It is really important that you realize that if you are spending your time on negativity, blaming, and excuses, things likely won't change. If you instead spend your energy on something positive and finding your solutions, you'll actually manifest the change. Most of us have read the book, "The Secret." If you interview the most successful people in the world, you will find that most of them believe in the power of manifestation. You will find, however, that most successful people don't just believe in manifesting through dreaming or thinking, but actually are putting the ACTION behind the thinking.

I have heard so many people say that they created a vision board and just waited for everything to fall into place. I believe that you have to take deliberate action toward your dreams and your goals to actually realize them! Don't blame. Don't make excuses. Just take deliberate and relentless action toward your goals.

Over the past few years after I left financial planning, we were really hoping that Mike's business would do well while we were building mine. Over those five years, his business did "just fine," but not nearly well enough when you considered how hard he was working. He was frustrated and spending hours and hours, but always felt like he was spinning his wheels. It was frustrating. There were tons of times that I wanted him to just give up and go back to a regular job. However, Mike DEFINITELY has what it takes to be an entrepreneur. Every time things got tough, he would say, "I haven't lost until I give up. I will keep doing what I know is right, and it will pay off." This past year, Mike didn't just have his best year ever. He had his best year ever times FOUR! He knew he was doing the right things, and he knew that it would pay off as long as he kept going.

If your ship doesn't come in, swim out
to meet it.
Jonathan Winters

Dealing with Things Out of Your Control

I was recently speaking to one of my clients who is opening a barre studio in California. God bless her. She has a great plan. She has a great spin on her concept. She has capital. She is hard working and very focused. This has been her plan for years, but I swear, it seems that every single obstacle that the city could throw at her, they have! They needed to approve her use of the space. They wanted to check for what type of noise she would create. They wanted to test parking and traffic patterns. Every time she thought she was through it, someone would tell her about another hoop that they would make her jump through.

We were having a conversation a few weeks ago, and she said that a long-time business owner told it to her in a way that she completely understood. As an entrepreneur, you need to be ready, willing, and able to do whatever it takes to power past a problem. It may be money. It may be hard work. It may be pure perseverance. As long as you keep going, you'll normally succeed.

But you need to CONSTANTLY be evaluating:

- Where are you today?
- Where do you want to go?
- What is the best way to get there?
- What obstacles do you anticipate facing?
- How will you get around them?

As long as you plan for the fact that there WILL be bumps in the road, you aren't surprised or disappointed when they arise.

Finding Your Strengths.
- What are you good at?
- What will you not do, even if your business depends on it?
- What do you love to do?

- If you were to ask 10 people around you what they see as your biggest strength, what would they say?
- What would they say that you do better than most?

This is what would be called your Unique Ability or Zone of Genius. Often, if you are operating in your Zone of Genius, you will be more successful than if you are forcing yourself to do things that you aren't good at. When I first started financial planning, my boss was working with Dan Sullivan, "The Strategic Coach." He was the first person I ever heard talking about Unique Abilities, and his teachings challenged everything I had ever heard about mastery.

Rather than trying to force yourself to do or learn things that aren't in your strengths, focus instead on spending your time doing things that you are good at. You'll get more done and be more successful. For example, if one of your marketing strategies is to run Facebook ads, but you aren't good with technology and reviewing metrics, it is likely not the highest and best use of your time to be learning Facebook ads to run them yourself.

Whereas if you are the visionary of your business and are able to step back and look at your business with a critical eye and evaluate what needs to be done next, that is a good use of your time. For me, I have two significant unique abilities. First, I have a very strategic and critical eye. I am able to look at business problems and identify the areas for improvement. Second, I am able to take complicated strategies and boil them down to their essence and explain them in a way that people can understand. I also DO have a very logistical and technical mind, so I love developing systems.

I am NOT the best sales person, however. I am not someone who is great with going up and talking to people I don't know. I am actually a bit of an introvert. I am not the best with managing a staff. I KNOW these things, and if I want to be a successful business owner, I had to learn that it was NOT the best use of my time and energy to waste my time trying to master those tasks vs. hiring those tasks out to my staff. Now, I am better able to spend my time doing things that I like and am good at, and I hire people to do the things that I DON'T do well.

Also, I learned that the best way to get the behaviors I wanted was to INCENTIVIZE the behaviors that I wanted. We'll get into this further when we get into the Staffing chapter, but what you need to know now is this:

- What are your zones of genius?
- What do you NOT do well?

Do The Work:
Skills Identifier

Ask 10 people that know you well, (ideally in both a personal and business setting), what do I do really well?

_____

_____

_____

Please be honest. This is important to the success of my business. What do you feel I do NOT do well that maybe I would be better served hiring someone else to do for me? If you are afraid that people won't be honest to your face, or you are concerned that you won't be able to take the feedback, please send it via email.

_____

_____

_____

Copy this page and give it to 10 people who know you well and ask them the things they feel you do best and the things they feel you should hire others to help you with.

Do more of what makes you happy –
Ralph Waldo Emerson

CHAPTER 2:
Goal Setting for Success

*Life is what happens to you when you are
busy making other plans.*
John Lennon

At some point in your life, I am guessing that you have been taught about setting goals. This book is meant to be a business book. One thing that I learned a few years ago is that if my life is out of balance, then my business won't be successful.

I often get busy in my life and business. When I do, I find that I let other aspects of my life slip, in particular my own fitness routine and my time with friends. I can always tell if my life is in balance and I'm meeting all my needs based on my weight. I can fluctuate 5-10 pounds at any given time just based on my habits outside of my business!

So, before you get ready to start a business, I want you to identify the things that are important to you and your life. This way, when you are moving forward in your business, you can identify when your life is out of balance. This next chapter will be all about your LIFE goals!

One of my and my husband, Mike's, New Year's traditions has been to sit down and do a year in review of the prior year and establish our goals for the next year. This tends to be a really good exercise for us. We enjoy reviewing our successes (our failures not so much) and looking toward to the New Year with a renewed sense of possibility.

It is also a great time to determine if we are on the same page. You can always tell where someone's heart is by their goals and their checkbook. However, one unfortunate observation we have made over the past year or two is that we don't set and review our goals often enough. I have a horrible history of writing down my goals and saving them in a file on my computer or putting them on my bulletin board and never really looking at them again.

As I have really been researching and reviewing goal setting success, I have learned so much about what makes someone more successful. So, as you start on this new journey, I want to challenge you to review your goal setting (and goal reviewing) experience. You need to know where you want to go to know if you are going in the right direction!

You've likely heard the analogy that you climb all the way up a ladder and get to the top only to find out the ladder was leaning against the wrong wall. Ideally, you will always be very conscious about where you have come from and where you are going.

There was a recent study of Harvard MBA students. They wanted to determine how some of the most successful people in the world both set and achieved their goals. In reviewing the class, they found that only 13% of the class had actually identified their goals. Of the entire class, only 3% of the class (of super smart and successful people) wrote their goals down. Do you know what was fascinating about it all? The 13% of the class who had goals but did not write them down happened to be earning twice the amount of the 84% who had no goals. The 3% who had written goals were earning, on average, ten times as much as the other 97% of the class combined!

Every single time I go to a business coaching event, the leader takes the time to have all the participants write down their goals. The business coach understands that they can't help you achieve your goals if you haven't identified what they are. It is an important exercise to really identify WHERE you want to go!

If you don't identify where you want to go, it's very likely that this time next year, you'll be in a very similar place to where you are today - with no real progress!

You can go to work, or you can be the boss.
You choose.
Amy Mewborn

SMART GOALS

Have you heard the acronym SMART goals? SMART goals are goals that follow a specific set of guidelines and have a higher likelihood of attainment.

SMART stands for:
- Specific
- Measurable
- Achievable
- Realistic
- Time Bound

Before you start identifying your goals, we want to set you up for the highest likelihood of goal attainment. So, let's really write some SMART goals!

Specific:
Your goal should be as specific as possible. What is the goal? Tell me specifically what it is. For example, if your goal is to lose weight, you don't want to say that your goal is to lose weight. You want to say that your goal is to lose 10 pounds! Be specific – HOW MUCH?

List Your Goal. WHAT is the goal?

_____

_____

_____

Measurable:
Along the line of specific becomes measurable. If you set the goal to "lose weight," and you lose one pound, technically you achieved your goal. However, I would guess that very few people set the goal to lose one pound. Set a goal that you can measure (or keep score against). Again, with our goal above – If I said, "I want to lose 10 pounds, I can constantly measure how close or how far I am from achieving that goal based on the number on a scale!

How will you measure the goal?

_____

_____

_____

Achievable:
This is simple. Be realistic. Your goal should be a stretch. It should be something that you have to work to achieve, but it should be attainable and realistic. For example, if your goal is to lose weight, to lose 80 pounds, and you only weigh 160 pounds, that is likely not attainable (or wise).

How will you achieve this goal?

_____

_____

_____

Realistic:
Along with the Achievable and Attainable, the goal must be realistic. Your goal to lose 10 pounds may be completely attainable, but if you want to lose 10 pounds in the next two days, that is likely not realistic. Much of "realistic" is based on whether or not it is achievable in the time frame allotted!

Is this goal realistic?

_____

_____

_____

Time Bound:

What is the time frame in which you would like to achieve this goal? You have likely heard the phrase, "a goal is a dream with a deadline." If you do not have a timeline for when you want to achieve your goals, then your goals just keep getting pushed back, and maybe "one day," you'll get it done! Your deadline needs to be achievable and realistic, but again, it should push you!

What is the time frame to achieve this goal?

_____

_____

_____

Practical Application:
Getting My CFP – I Really Didn't Want To.

Have you ever noticed that the amount of time you allot for something is normally the amount of time that it takes? When I started my certified financial planning program, I really had a hard time committing to it. Honestly, the reason is, I really wasn't that interested in it at the time. It was a large commitment of my time and energy, and I was doing it to make my boss happy at the time - not really because I wanted to do it.

The Certified Financial Planner program is a five-year program - with five major courses, each needing to be passed before you go on to the next portion! The average pass rate at the time I took the course was only about 60% on the first try.

Well, I started my CFP program in 2002. I knew that I had five years to get it done. I completed the first course in less than 6 months, but because my heart wasn't in it, I really struggled to start the second course. So you know what? I didn't - for almost 4 years! Even if you're not a math major, you may see my problem. I had five years to complete the entire program! In the entire 4.5 years prior, I had ONLY completed the first of five courses. So guess what? I had a HUGE deadline coming up. I had 6 months to complete FOUR courses - in addition to my full time job! So you know what happened next? I worked my butt off - doing pretty much nothing other than work and study. To make a long story short, I studied hard and passed each course. I passed my multi-day exam, and I completed the program to achieve my Certified Financial Planner Certificate.

Now, I'll tell you, this was NOT the way to complete the program, but I needed a deadline! I needed a reason to have to get it done! I needed a time that it needed to be completed by - otherwise, I still may not have finished it today!

Most of us don't make a change until either the deadline is upon us or the current situation has become SO painful that we can't stand to stay where we are. So today, I want you to sit down, and let's create this list of goals!

Do The Work:

So before you go any further, I want you to determine the following:

If we were sitting here next year and this had been a wildly successful year, what would have happened to make it a great year? Tell it to me as a story!

Do The Work:

Now that you've told me this story, I want you to create a list of different types of goals. If you don't have three types of each goal, or a certain area is not a goal for you, that is totally fine.

I want you to make a list of these goals. I want you to write these goals.

- o List Three Health Goals
- o List Three Professional Achievement Goals
- o List Three Educational Goals
- o List Three Spiritual Goals
- o List Three Personal/Relational Goals

Whatever your goals are, identify them! WRITE THEM DOWN!

Three Health Goals:

_____

_____

_____

Three Professional Achievement Goals:

_____

_____

_____

Three Spiritual Goals:

_____

_____

_____

Three Personal/Relational Goals:

_____

_____

_____

Ok have you done it? Have you written your goals down?

Now, I want you to review the goals.

- Are they SMART goals?
- Are they Specific?
- Can you Measure them?
- Are they Attainable?
- Are they Realistic?
- Is there a Time by which they will each be completed?

Within Your Heart, Keep One Secret Spot
Where Your Dreams May Go
Whitney Johnson

Based on the goals and the timelines, identify what needs to get done first.

- What has an actual deadline?
- If you do not have deadlines assigned to each goal, I want you to assign a SPECIFIC deadline to each and e-very goal
- When will you be out of that job you hate?

- When will you start that new business you've been dreaming of?
- When will you get to where you want to go?
- Write those down.

Now that you have goals and deadlines, let's identify the action items necessary to achieve these goals. Do you need a new education? Do you need to make a phone call and register for something? WHAT specifically do you need to do to make this happen?

Goal	Deadline	Action Steps

Ok, now that you have identified what you need to do, when you need to do it by, and specifically what actions need to be taken, let's talk about how you're actually going to get it done!

Are you like me? Some days you wake up and are so overwhelmed by your schedule or what you need to get done that you almost feel frozen and unable to complete anything?

When I was helping clients in financial planning, I knew how important the action steps were to goal attainment. I actually created an entire online tool to help clients achieve their goal. It was called the Next Step Checklist! In MY life, however, I often felt paralyzed by my to-do list - and unable to move - until I stepped back and created a system that helped me identify the things I needed to do and HOW to get them done!

I will tell you that one of the most common habits of successful people is that they schedule their week on Sunday, or they make their to-do list the day prior. So, for example, in finance, I was making my to-do list for the following week before I left the office on Friday. This helped me close the loop between what was completed that week and what needed my immediate attention the following week! Often in our personal lives, however, we fight order and systems - feeling like they are stifling us! Until one day we wake up and realize an entire month has gone by and we didn't accomplish what we had hoped.

As an entrepreneur, I have found that if I sit down Sunday night I can take just 15-20 minutes and schedule out all the things I want to accomplish in my week. I literally block them as appointments in my ical! This way when I walk out of teaching classes on Monday afternoon, I have a list of the 10 things I want to accomplish before the end of my work day. If something doesn't get done, I move it into the following day. Then when I get up on Tuesday morning, I can jump out of bed, make my cup of coffee and get right to work - rather than taking an hour (or more) piddling in my social media, email, and every other distraction, while I'm trying to decide what to tackle first!

Take that list of goals, action items, and deadlines and actually put them in your calendar! Create a date with yourself and a commitment with yourself to get it DONE! If you have decided it is the time to start your new life, take action. Don't wait another moment! This is the year that you are going to finally make a change and build the life you've always dreamed of!

I used to create these crazy long to do lists. They were a great way for me to get things out of my brain and onto paper and greatly increased the likelihood that I would actually do what I had been thinking about. Unfortunately, I would often find that my to-do list just became longer and longer, and I was so focused on the stuff at the end of the to-do list (the new stuff) that I would completely forget about or ignore the top of the to-do list!

So one day, once I had gone to an electronic calendar, I found something else that worked a whole lot better for me! I now actually make every single to do an appointment. It gets a realistic time frame on my calendar, and if something happens, and I don't get to it today, I just drag it to tomorrow (or another date in the future). I sometimes find that I put something on the calendar to get it out of my head, and there is no real benefit to actually achieving that task. Great! I get to delete it, but I also then am forced to prioritize my day a little bit better. Throughout the day, I am constantly looking at my calendar and determining what needs to be done. If something is less important today, I just move it to tomorrow! This method really helps me stay on point and stay focused on what is important vs. the ever growing to do list!

Work Life Balance

Ok, we're going to tackle a tough subject for women! I will touch on this subject a few times in this book because I feel it is SO important! I have spent a number of years running a fitness business, but despite being in a position of health, fitness, and motivation of others, I find that my physical, mental, emotional, spiritual, and relational health are the first things to suffer! You see, as a business owner, there is ALWAYS something to do. I could sit here all day long and find more and more to do.

---

*You can have it all, as long as you don't
do it all.
Unknown*

The problem is that I often forget that I can have it all as long as I don't believe I have to do it all. In addition, I need to remember that if I don't get "it" (whatever "it" is) done, the world will definitely not come to an end! Many entrepreneurs are idea people. They can be sitting there over dinner and come up with a great idea that they just HAVE to implement now. I never leave a vacation without at least one new idea on how to better my business. So after a vacation, in addition to all the items that my staff has added to my to do list, I have added to it myself with new tasks and projects!

After over 20 years of business, finance, and planning, I still believe in setting annual goals. But I now believe that if you really want to achieve your goals, your goals need to be more bite-sized.

When you are setting your annual goals, you also need these goals to be something that you can attain and feel a moment of success. Maybe rather than focusing on reaching big goals, you could break those goals down into more small, measurable goals.

Are you like me? I write down these goals, but I used to put them away in a file and didn't ever look at them again until the end of the year. I would accomplish some of them, but never have given others a second thought. So maybe rather than setting large, annual goals, consider having a series of goals just for each month.

Breaking through your blocks:

1. What are you good at?

2. What are you passionate about? If you could make money doing any business, what would it be?

3. What need do you see in the world that you think you could solve?

4. What do you do best? In an ideal world, you would do only that. Anything else you are doing is a disservice to the business.

Do what you're good at, and do it over and over until you make a ton of money, then use the money to have fun and help people.

Dream Life

Tell me about your dream month?
   a. What days/times/weeks would you work?
   b. What would you do in your time off?

What would you do with an extra $10,000 per month?

_____

_____

_____

What is holding you back from achieving these goals?

_____

_____

_____

What is the number one challenge you need to overcome?

_____

_____

_____

What is keeping you from overcoming that challenge?

_____

_____

_____

How would your life change by overcoming this challenge?

_____

_____

_____

Now that you know where you want to go, let's identify HOW you're going to get there. Let's start writing your business plan!

Opportunities may not always be obvious,
but they are always there.
Cathie Black

CHAPTER 3:
Getting Your Personal Financial House in Order

When you get ready to open your own business, you will find that your business finances and your personal finances are directly intertwined. If you have put yourself in danger on one side of your finances, you will likely experience added stress in the other. The safety of your business and the financial security of your life are dependent on you making good decisions!

One of the biggest and simplest pieces of advice that I can give you is to not let your lifestyle get too out of control. You never know all the things that can go wrong, so you want to make sure that you have a strong cash reserve and that you could make the payments even under less than ideal circumstances. Let me tell you a personal story...

Practical Application

I mentioned in the last chapter how I have stressed over our large house over the past ten years. Mike and I bought our new house in 2005. We were both employed, had steady paychecks, were saving good money toward retirement every year, and had a fairly healthy cash reserve. Our payment on our new house was over $7,000 per month, and our total monthly expenses were about $15,000 - $20,000 a month. As long as we were both working, we were just fine and there were no concerns.

However, about a month and a half after we moved into our new house, Mike's company was bought out, and 25% of the company was laid off. Although we had a decent cash reserve, for the type of expenses we had taken on, the cash reserve would never take care of us for 6 months! Fortunately, we still had my income, and Mike used his severance package to take the opportunity to become self-employed and become a Realtor.

In this moment, we were ok, but over the next 10 years, we had more than our fair share of stresses and anxieties over our ridiculously high bills and monthly obligations. Later in this chapter, I'll tell you the time it really created stress, but as you are reading this chapter, hear these words – don't let your expenses get out of control. You need to always have control over both your personal and business finances; otherwise, there will be many sleepless nights in your business future!

Also, please remember that just because you have a certain level of income today, you may not always have that much coming in every year (especially if your income is based on sales, commissions, or profits of a business). When Mike was laid off, we had about $75,000 in savings. Based on our expenses, we really should have had about $120,000. As you are preparing to launch a business, you MUST have a personal cash reserve. Otherwise you are setting yourself up to fail.

As we move forward in this chapter, I will cover your monthly income and expenses. I encourage you to try to build a savings account that will cover six months of your entire set of expenses. This will give you some stability and will help protect you against unanticipated expenses and needs!

There are two common clichés/schools of thought about how to run your business when you're first starting. They are both widely accepted, and they each have their perks. I will tell you that only one, however, will help you build a long-term business indefinitely.

- Fake It Till You Make It
- Lead with Revenue

Fake It Till You Make It

When I started in financial planning, the sales managers were ALL about Fake It Till You Make It. They believed that when you were out meeting with clients, even if you were 24 years old, fresh out of college, you needed to be driving a really nice car and dressed to the nines. Imagine fifty new 24-year olds all parking their Mercedes in the parking lot – when only five to ten of them were actually going to make it in the business. It probably wasn't the best lesson!

Today in the day of Real Housewives, celebrity, and personal branding, image is becoming increasingly important. I remember reading Barbara Corcoran's book, "Shark Tales," and she talked about how she was all for "Fake It Till You Make It." She felt that her expensive coat was something that set her apart (and made her feel more successful). In her case, it may have worked. However, I can tell you that I feel this is dangerous advice! In my years as a financial advisor, I know a lot of sales people who had been sold on the Fake It Till You Make It mentality, and they found themselves further and further in debt. The common statement from a sales or business person with this mentality is that they just need to work harder and sell more to make up for it. I can tell you that this is a slippery slope. If this IS the direction someone follows, it will create a lot of stress and anxiety to avoid ending up in debt over your status symbols.

I'm not saying you can't have one amazing "power outfit" that you pull out for big events, conferences, etc. You can't show up and inspire confidence in old tattered clothes or miss a client meeting because you're driving around in a car that won't start. Be careful though... The Fake It Till You Make It Mindset is NOT sustainable in the long term unless you start making enough money to stop faking it!

Lead with Revenue

The second financial school of thought is Lead with Revenue. I feel that this is a much safer, long-term financial strategy.

As I progressed in finance, I met hundreds of wildly successful business owners who took a very different path. The most successful owners that were raised by families of business owners were often the most conservative. They maintained significant cash reserves and believed that you "Lead with Revenue," which means that you don't buy something or invest in something unless there is revenue to pay for it.

Now obviously this isn't always practical. Most business owners have needed a credit card, a business loan, or a line of credit at some point in their business, whether it was their start up, their expansion, or to get them through a downturn in the business, but the difference is in the mentality.

If you are always looking to generate more revenue before you expand, you'll likely never get in trouble for over extending yourself financially! You may not grow as fast as you had hoped or imagined, but you will also not find yourself drowning in debt or bills that you can't sustain!

We'll get into this more in this chapter, but I want you to keep these two financial mindsets in mind as we discuss both your business and your personal financial situation.

Understand Your Personal Finances.

I have worked with two types of entrepreneurs- those who want to know EVERY detail of their finances, and those that have no idea at all what their books look like.

As an entrepreneur, the success of your business is directly related to how well you keep track of your finances – both personal and business!

Why is this important? It's simple…

o   Clarity comes from information. The more you understand, the clearer you become!

o   Having your personal finances in order will allow you to implement your business strategies with confidence and without a stressful struggle that can paralyze your business growth.

o   When you worry about your finances, it creates a TON of stress.   You can't make clear, informed, unemotional decisions, and ultimately, you can't successfully run your business.

o   If you understand your finances, you can better understand and amend your capital needs as business circumstances change.   I have worked with an advisor in the past that calls this to "pivot."   When you are running a business, it is guaranteed that things will change. You need to be able to review your financials and make a good decision – or "pivot" in another direction if necessary!

o   The more you understand your finances, the more clearly you can see opportunities!

o   When you are first opening your business, it may be difficult to get a business loan or other type of business credit, but if you have excellent personal credit, you may be able to get personal loans to see your business though start up or a business crisis. (If you do personal loans, be aware that they open you up to liability to creditors.)

Get CLEAR On Your Finances – Understanding Your Net Worth

Before we go any further in business finances, let's make sure that you fully understand your personal financial situation. Your Net Worth is one of the first measures of your financial health. Simply put, your **net worth** is: the value of your ASSETS minus your LIABILITIES.

To measure your net worth, add up all of your assets.

Assets Include Your:
- House
- Autos
- Checking Accounts
- Savings Accounts
- Stocks
- Bonds
- Mutual Funds
- Retirement Plans
- Any other personal property

Then add up all of your liabilities.

Liabilities Include Your:
- Mortgage
- Auto Loans
- Student Loans
- Credit Card Debt
- Personal Loans

Now, subtract the total liability amount from the asset amount and you'll know your net worth.

Calculate your net worth with the spreadsheet below:
Balance Sheet

Current Assets	Amount
Cash/Checking Account	
Savings Account/CD/Money Market	
Stocks/Bonds	
Retirement Accounts	
Home	
Automobiles	
Personal Property	
Other Assets	
Other Assets	
Total Assets	
Current Liabilities	**Amount**
Mortgage	
Auto Loans	
Student Loans	
Credit Cards/Lines of Credit	
Other Liabilities	
Other Liabilities	
Total Liabilities	
Total Net Worth	

Did you do it? Was your net worth a positive or a negative number? If you have a negative net worth right now, don't panic. First, it is common for younger people to have a negative number. Second, if you own real estate that has depreciated since you purchased it, you may have a negative number that may not be the norm. However, no matter what any advisor says, it never hurts to know your numbers. Your numbers will be a measure of the health of your finances and your business.

If your net worth is low or negative, you now know you need to increase your savings and decrease your spending in order to improve your net worth. Just for reference, typical retirement goals require you to save around ten percent of your gross yearly income.

Practical Application

In 2010 when I left corporate America, Mike and I had our home and a rental home both in San Diego. We had no credit card debt. We had no student loans, and we had one car payment. We had savings accounts. We had investments, and we had retirement account. However, our largest assets were our personal residence and our rental property. Due to the significant housing downturn, our net worth very quickly went from over $400,000 in the positive to almost $200,000 in a very short period of time.

Thank goodness we didn't need to get financing to open the first studio. If we had, I'm sure they never would have considered us! As it is, it's pretty unbelievable that we were able to get a commercial landlord to rent to us! However, because of the circumstances of our debt, there was very little we could do to better our net worth at the time, except to keep saving, keep building assets, and to pay down our car and mortgages!

The only option we had was to keep our heads down, keep making money, saving money, and paying down debt. Just five years later, things were very different. Instead of having a negative net worth of almost $200,000, we had built our savings, built our investments, built our businesses, and our real estate had improved. Our net worth had increased to over $500,000. This is a change of over $700,000 in just five years. Honestly, looking back, we could have done even better had we been more frugal!

If you aren't happy with your net worth, you have the potential to make a change! Remember, complaining about your circumstances won't change them. The only thing you can do is make decisions that will better you and your finances!

As you get into your 30's and 40's, it is important to begin planning for retirement, so if your net worth is still negative, make a concerted effort to increase income and decrease spending in order to improve your net worth.

Here are some of the "easiest" ways to increase your net worth:

Build a Cash Reserve

Your cash reserve will be your account that is liquid and least susceptible to market fluctuations. A cash reserve should be kept in a savings account or a money market account. These types of investment will not typically fluctuate with the market, and they are both normally 100% available to you immediately if you need the money.

**Note – a money market account is a very short-term bond account. They do experience very minimal market fluctuation, but often experience slightly higher rates of return than a savings account will. However, because these are normally mutual funds, it may take three days for the funds to "settle."

Save or Make Money

Before you leave a job and open a business, you want to make sure that you fully understand how much you need to make on a monthly basis.

Attached you will find a Profit and Loss statement, otherwise known as an Income and Expense statement. I will be calling this a P&L Statement. You will find three columns, and we call these your Silver, Gold, and Platinum Standard of Living.

Income and Expense Calculator

Income Sources	Silver	Gold	Platinum
Employment Income			
Self-Employment Income			
Spouse Income			
Other Income			
Other Income			
TOTAL INCOME			
Fixed Expenses			
Taxes			
Housing			
Auto Payments			
Health Insurance			
Auto Insurance			
Other Insurance			
Gas and Electric			
Water			
Trash			
Phone			
Internet			
Food, Groceries, etc			
Credit Card Payments			
Other Loan Payments			
Savings			
Retirement Savings			
Other Fixed:			
Other Fixed:			
TOTAL FIXED EXPENSES			
Discretionary Expenses			
Travel			
Dining and Entertainment			
Gifts			
Shopping, hobbies, etc			
Other discretionary:			
Other discretionary:			
TOTALDISCRETIONARY EXPENSES			
TOTAL EXPENSES			
TOTAL NET INCOME			

For Silver, you will enter all the ESSENTIAL expenses. These include rent/mortgage, car payments, insurance payments, food, and other things that you can't do without. For Gold, you will start to budget toward paying down debt - dining out, travel, and other discretionary expenses that are important to you, but not absolutely necessary. You may not be able to do everything you wish, but your Gold Standard is when you have enough money to start adding "fun" back into your life!

For Platinum, put together your practical dream life (Oxymoron, right?), but imagine if you were traveling a few times a year, saving for lifestyle goals, making extra payments, etc. This is how much you will need to be making to live the life you really are aspiring to. If you need to add more money to your savings account, you have a couple of options. You can either cut back on your expenses, or make more money. Some people do a combination of both.

Before you leave a job and open a business, you want to make sure that you fully understand how much you need to make on a monthly basis. You also must have a savings account or cash reserve. It will be impossible to launch a business and make good decisions if every decision means the difference between having plenty or not having enough money to feed your family.

Hopefully your current net income is a positive number – meaning that you have more income than you need and have money available to save. If so, great! Determine how much more you can be saving toward your short and long-term goals and start paying yourself that amount out of every single check before it goes into your checking account. Anyone who has amassed a strong retirement fund will tell you that they did it by saving toward their retirement from their GROSS income each month, not their net income after expenses. If you wait to save from your net income, you will find that there is never really any "net income" left!

If you need to add more money to your savings account, you have a couple of options. You can either cut back on your expenses, or make more money. Some people do a combination of both. For today, I would encourage you to go through the expense statement and see what you can cut from your monthly budget for a little while. For example, when Mike and I get busy (and lazy) we eat out over 50% of our meals. When we need to cut back on expenses, we go to Costco and mass prepare a number of meals, literally saving HUNDREDS of dollars each week! We also cut back on our cable plans and other entertainment.

Mike is an avid golfer. So, if money is tight at any given time, he skips some of his golf games. Or maybe I have to pass on that latte, new sweater, or new pair of shoes. I'd guess that you have some things in your expenses that would be pretty easy to cut out. These are the things that you could cut out and really wouldn't even miss them. List them and determine if that feels like a good fit for achieving your goals. Then once you have cut out the things you wouldn't really miss, go back through again. Is there anything else in your monthly or annual expenses that you could cut out (even if these may be a bit more painful). Commit to making real financial changes. Start saving first for your goals, and see if you can get to work increasing your cash reserve!

Travel Budget

This may or may not apply to you, but for most people that I know that are in my age group or younger – it totally applies. Your travel budget is likely a large expense that can be reduced! When income is flowing, Mike and I LOVE to travel. Whether it is a weekend getaway to Palm Springs or a two-week trip to an all-inclusive resort in Cabo, our travel budget is absolutely one of our largest expenses of the year other than housing, food, and automobiles.

If you are serious about starting a business and need to save some money, consider cutting back on your travel for a couple of years. I believe that you will find that after running your business a year or two, it will afford you the freedom and income to be able to travel MORE, but you really do need to have a cash reserve and a sustainable lifestyle leading up to opening your business and in that first year in business!

Add up how much you have spent on travel over the past year, and see if you can allocate even half of that to your new business fund! If you can reduce the lattes, the dining out, entertainment, shopping, and travel, I believe you will find that your business fund may grow quickly!

Do the Work:

List ten places that you can reduce your expenses and an estimate of how much you can save over the next year.

_____

_____

_____

_____

_____

_____

_____

_____

_____

_____

_____

Make Sure You Have Good Credit

At some point, you're likely going to need some type of credit to finance your business. Maybe you need to put a business trip on your credit card. You may need to invest in inventory or training. You may have an unexpected tax bill. You may decide to expand, or maybe you need extra money to meet payroll to keep the business running in lean times.

Having access to credit may be imperative to getting you through any one of these situations. Making these investments on credit may be required, and you need access to credit when it has the potential to help you make MORE money and move forward. Whether you are getting credit through the business or you are accessing credit personally, the first thing that a potential creditor will check is your credit score.

Your credit score is comprised by a few different things:

- Payment History – the first thing any lender wants to know is whether or not you have a history of paying your bills on time. If you don't pay your bills on time, then what is the likelihood you will pay them on time? They also want to know if you have ever defaulted on past loans. Again, if you have a history of not repaying a past creditor, what is the likelihood that you wouldn't repay them?
- Amounts Owed – Do you have $50,000 in credit available to you, with $50,000 in liabilities? This will tell a lender that you are likely a higher risk borrower. Whereas, if you have $50,000 in credit available but are only using $5,000 of it, then you probably don't need the credit very much at that particular time - meaning you are likely a low risk borrower.
- Length of Credit History – Generally, the longer your credit history, the higher your score. If you have had credit available and have used it responsibly, you likely will have a higher score
- Types of credit in use – the credit bureaus will look at whether or not you have different types of credit. Do you have a mortgage, an auto loan, and some credit cards, or do you only have $100,000 in credit card lines available? If you only have revolving credit (things like credit cards), that is considered a higher risk.
- New credit – How much of your credit is new credit? Have you been out applying for a number of new credit cards all at one time? If so, credit bureaus will immediately reduce your score, and a lender will wonder what is going on in your life that is causing the need for a large amount of new credit. With these circumstances, you will likely find that you are unable to get credit at that time!

That said, you want to find out beforehand what your credit score is like. The three major credit bureaus where you can request your credit score and credit report are:

- o Equifax: http://www.equifax.com
- o Experian: http://www.experian.com
- o TransUnion: http://www.transunion.com

Understand Your Finances BEFORE You Leave a Secure Job.

Hopefully now you have a clear picture of your current financial situation. Now that you know where you stand, it is time to explore your options and plan accordingly.

If you have a significant other, it is imperative that you both determine that you are ready to move forward with a new business and how. For simplicity's sake, I will start addressing you here as if you have a spouse, but no matter what the relationship, if you share finances or a home, it is important that both are on the same page. Talk with your spouse about your financial situation and how to best pursue your new business idea.

- Do you think you can continue working your full-time job while starting your business on the side?

- Can you afford to go part-time and really pour your energy into your new business idea?

- Can you afford to leave your job completely and launch a new business?

Your new business may take more time and energy than you anticipate. If it does, how will you pick up the slack? To help you make a well-thought out decision, be sure you take the following things into consideration:

- If you currently have a job, will there be enough money coming in without you working or without you making money from your business right away?
- Will your family be supportive of you working long hours?
- Will your family lose access to health insurance if you leave a job?
- Will you need to hire additional child care or other home help in order to get everything done?
- Will there still be money to save toward retirement goals or other financial needs?
- Will your family be ok with the tradeoff that you may not be doing a ton of leisure travel for the first few months while you are launching your new business?
- What are the long term goals of your new life?

Practical Application

When I realized I was unhappy in my career, I came home and told Mike (my husband) that I wanted to leave my six figure job! At the time, I was the primary breadwinner in our family, and we were dependent on my income. Mike went and visited studios with me. He sat with me as we determined financial needs. He sat with me as we determined what we could cut from our bills. Although he had a lot to lose from me leaving my job, he was not only supportive, but he pretty much dropped everything for a couple of months to help me launch! The success of each of our businesses is because we operate as a team and support each other!

If you are serious about opening your own business, it is imperative that your partner and family understand and agree that some sacrifices will have to be made in order to make it successful. You may not be available to make dinner, pick up the kids, or any number of things that may be part of your normal routine.

If your spouse and/or family are not supportive of your goals, the time to seek counseling or to discuss the ramifications of this decision is *before* you start your business, not after the resentment builds and creates relationship problems!

Now you have a clear picture of what your financial situation is. You know where you stand, and now it's time to explore what your options are and plan accordingly.

Pay Off Debt

If you have any debt prior to leaving a steady job or starting your own business, consider trying to get rid of it before you give up that steady paycheck! Consumer debt (credit cards) is one of the most common reasons people stay at their jobs when they want to make a transition to business ownership. In most cases, debt *should* be the first thing addressed as you start your new business. While you're still at your job, pay off as much debt as you possibly can. Most financial advisors agree that it's best to pay off credit cards, even if you have to use your savings to do so (**Note**: consult with your financial advisor about your best options for reducing debt). Imagine having $20,000 in a savings account earning 0%, but paying 15% - 28% interest on a $5,000 credit card balance each and every month.

One thing you'll also hear from financial advisors to reduce your debt is to not add any new debt. This may mean that this year you can't afford a new car. It may also mean that you have to forego new furniture, carpeting, or a vacation that you were really looking forward to. If you are struggling to determine what is absolutely necessary to your life, ask someone you trust. They will often hold up a mirror and tell you that you don't really need that new watch, a new piece of jewelry, or most of the things you may think you need. If you do not have a financial advisor, find a trusted friend who has built wealth or a business! Ask them if they will mentor you in your new goal. Often times, you'll be surprised to find that many successful business owners want to pass on their wisdom to someone else! There are many very famous and successful business owners who have served as mentor to others. Often, all you have to do is ask.

In additions to paying off your debt, you want to make sure you have some savings in your bank account. It is wise to have a cushion of at least 3-6 months of your living expenses in your savings account *before* starting your business. If you can manage a year's income in savings, even better. Your savings should be in an account that is accessible, but not to be touched until absolutely necessary.

Let's take a look at what it looks like to cut back on your expenses...

Jennifer knows that she wants to launch a new business soon. She thinks she may need financing, but she is also unsure of what to do. She has determined that she should try to save more money, pay off her debt, and use her home equity to get a line of credit.

When she needed a new car, she bypassed the expensive car that she had really been dreaming about. Instead, she went with a cost-effective, practical car that required less maintenance. She allocated her travel budget to her new business and stopped going out for dinner and drinks with her friends to build a nest egg for her goal.

You could start a small personal service business such as tutoring, teaching fitness classes, or something else that you know how to do in order to make some extra money.

When my husband and I were getting ready to open our first fitness studio, we really cut back on our dining out, we didn't travel, and we cleaned out our house and re-allocated resources to the business, both tangibly and financially.

Think of ways you can add money to your savings account.

Are you willing to lower your expenses? Where can you cut back?

_____

_____

_____

Would you rather pick up some extra work? List some ways you can make more money.

_____

_____

_____

Keep Your Insurance Coverage

When you start your own business, it is important that you consider what type of benefits you are going to lose, and what benefits you really need. I'm not taking about box seats to the race track, or an expensive health club membership (but if you're at the point in your business, go for it). I'm talking health insurance, paid vacations, and retirement plans. The great news is that you have options as a self-employed worker to find adequate alternatives for you and your family.

Health Insurance

If you've been working a corporate job and you're thinking about leaving, find out what your options are for health insurance. In some instances, your employer's group health insurance coverage can be converted into individual coverage.

Based on your employer, you may be able to get COBRA coverage, individual health insurance, and coverage through the Affordable Care Act. Before you leave a steady job with benefits, don't forego health insurance as a way to save money!!!

Practical Application

When I first started financial planning, I had a friend, Brian, who lost his job. He did not want to pay the $500 month for Cobra coverage for himself and his wife. They "needed" a new car, so they decided to buy a new car and go without insurance.

A couple of months later, he had a major illness and had to have an emergency surgery to have his gallbladder removed. Then a few months later, they found out his wife was pregnant. Neither had insurance, and they racked up hundreds of thousands of dollars in medical bills. They had to declare bankruptcy; they couldn't rent an apartment, and they couldn't get credit cards.

There would have been no way they could have ever gotten business financing. This was all due to buying a new car and trying to save themselves just $6,000 over the course of a year by foregoing health insurance! No one ever plans for emergency medical bills. It is imperative that you not pass on something you truly need for something you want. If you work for yourself, there are other options and organizations that may offer access to insurance to their members.

If you need a few places to start your search, check out these resources:

- o Your local Chamber of Commerce
- o The Small Business Association www.sba.gov
- o Affordable Care Act www.healthcare.gov

Additional Insurance

It's also smart to prepare for things you wouldn't necessarily plan for —accidents, illness, disasters, etc. Here are a few recommendations:

- o Consider disability insurance that covers you in the event that you're disabled and can no longer earn an income.
- o If you have a family, consider term life insurance that will leave money for your significant other or spouse, children, or other dependents who may rely on your income.
- o Look for health insurance policies that will cover medical bills that, otherwise not covered, could potentially wipe out your savings.

Keep Funding Your Retirement

If you're coming from a corporate gig, you may have contributed to a 401k retirement fund at your company (if they offered one). The 401k is a group investment plan that you have the option to participate in with your company. When you leave your company, you can take all the money you have contributed with you. If your employer matched contributions and those contributions have vested, you will be able to take those funds as well However, your 401k is NOT a savings account. If you are not yet 59 ½ years old, and you cash out the fund, there will be substantial penalties and taxes. So, what you can do rather than withdraw the money is roll it into another retirement account.

Small business owners and solopreneurs have a few options for how to keep a retirement account. Let's take a look... (**NOTE:** the information below is for general purpose only. It is strongly suggested that you contact a financial advisor for details that pertain to your specific situation.)

- o **An Individual Retirement Account** (IRA) allows you to put up to a certain amount of money annually ($5,000 as of 2011) into a retirement account and defer taxes on that amount, plus any income earned by the IRA account, until you start taking money out of the account. With an IRA, you can't take out money until you reach 59 ½ years old. Note that business owners may have an IRA account without offering it to their employees.
- o **A Simplified Employee Pensions (SEPs) and Savings Incentive Match Plans for Employees (SIMPLEs)** allow small business owners to contribute more annually to their retirement fun than the IRA allows. The employer sets up the SEP with a brokerage house, bank, or insurance company and sets the criteria for employee eligibility. The

employer determines what percentage of the employees' salary will be put into the account. Even though the company creates the account, each account is managed by the employee. The company makes contributions to the account on behalf of the employee. The company uses the SEP contribution as a tax deduction, and the employee doesn't pay taxes on the money until they withdraw it.

o The **SIMPLE** is similar to the SEP, with some notable exceptions. With the SIMPLE, the employee makes contributions from their paycheck to the retirement account and the company matches the contribution, to a maximum of three percent of the employee's salary. The maximum contribution levels to the SEP are much higher compared to the SIMPLE.

For many people, company benefits and a retirement plan are the primary reasons for continuing to work for someone else. Though there is much to be said about the value of a regular paycheck, company benefits, and a retirement plan; with wise planning and self-discipline, small business owners can thrive without their past corporate benefits.

Exercises for Success

When my husband and I were getting ready to open our first studio, we really cut back on our dining out, we didn't travel, and we re-allocated resources to the business, both tangibly and financially. We moved mirrors, sofas, tables, desks, and computers into the business. Everything that we didn't have to buy new allowed us to save money.

List five ways you can reduce expenses:

_____

_____

_____

_____

_____

List three ways you can increase income:

_____

_____

_____

Do you have anything laying around the house that you can sell and start building more cash?

_____

_____

_____

_____

Do you have any personal items that the business could use that could save you money in your start up?

_____

_____

_____

_____

_____

_____

CHAPTER 4:
How You Show Up

I believe in pink. I believe that laughing is the best calorie burner. I believe in kissing, kissing a lot. I believe in being strong when everything seems to be going wrong. I believe that happy girls are the prettiest girls. I believe that tomorrow is another day and I believe in miracles.
Audrey Hepburn

Putting Your Best Foot Forward

How You Show Up, How You Interact with Others, and How to Be Remembered (in a good way). I am starting and finishing this chapter with quotes by Audrey Hepburn, mainly because years later, her style, class, and the way she carried herself remains iconic and something that many women aspire to!

As we discuss style and personal branding, I want you to really consider how you are presently known, and how you want to be known. Be aware of the gap and determine how you want to change it. Whether you know it or not, you have a personal brand. Your personal brand is how you are seen by your family, your friends, your business associates, acquaintances, and even through your online presence!

My husband, Mike, is a BIG personality. He walks into a room and within minutes, everyone knows him, and many people LOVE him. And although most love his friendly, disarming personality, sometimes people don't understand his sense of humor and they walk away thinking he's crazy and want nothing to do with him. He is normally well dressed, and he is always SUPER warm and friendly. However, he is occasionally told that he is a bit too informal for the liking of some!

Now because of his warmth and exuberance (i.e. large mouth), he is always noticed! The problem is that sometimes his exuberance is a turn off. One dangerous aspect about Mike's personality is this - often everyone remembers him, but he never really remembers anyone. He is so busy being the life of the party and entertaining everyone that he often does not make real, lasting connections – which are really the key to business success.

Secondly, everyone may remember him (and not always in a good way). Mike's big personality makes him very memorable, but not everyone always likes him or remembers him positively.

*Imperfection is beauty, madness is genius
and it's better to be absolutely ridiculous
than absolutely boring.
Marilyn Monroe*

For me, I tend to be a bit (or a lot) more understated. I want to go in looking professional; I want to be remembered, but I will not be the one holding court with a group of 50 people all standing around me hanging on my every word. I'll be talking to 4-5 people at a time, trying to build relationships and really get to know people. I am always doing my best to remember people's faces and their names. I could meet you today and often see you on the street six months later and remember your face, your name, and something about you.

More often than not, people remember that they have met me or know me from somewhere, but don't really REMEMBER me. I tend to blend in to the crowd. I can't change the fact that I am an introvert at heart. It takes a lot of energy for me to be super outgoing at a party! I am also not one who is going to share a lot of me or my life with a bunch of strangers!

If given the perfect Saturday night, Mike and I would order in pizza, start a fire, open a great bottle of wine, and watch a Hallmark movie or talk about life. I'll never be the life of the party. However, I knew I was ready to up-level my business and needed to identify how I could be more memorable without having to change my personality.

About a year ago, I started working with a branding expert, and we really went over the elements of what makes a fabulous personal brand. What I found is that sometimes I needed to step up a bit and be a bit more adventurous! My favorite stores have always been Banana Republic, Lululemon, and White House Black Market. Although the quality of my clothes have always been excellent, I had a huge walk-in closet of black and gray, and really nothing that stands out! I learned that if I wanted to up-level my wardrobe, I needed to start venturing out a bit and investing in signature, unique pieces in bright colors and fabrics.

In doing a recent photo shoot, I picked out a gorgeous off-white, leather motorcycle jacket. It was classic but edgy. It was buttery soft and gorgeous. It was more expensive than I would normally have spent. Yet, it really fit the direction of my new personal brand. I thought about it for a week. I "visited" it four times over the next week. Then, I finally bit the bullet and spent over $500 on a single jacket!

You know what though, that one piece has gotten more compliments and has had people reaching out to me online or after a party talking about it for weeks to come. Sometimes, we get in a rut and just become very comfortable with our clothes or our routines.

As you are preparing for your new life in business, I want to ask you: who is the network you want to build (business owners, clients, community partners, vendors, etc.) and how do you want to show up with them?

Carry yourself like you know where you are going
Cathie Black

- Is your goal to be known as the girl in fitness apparel?
- Do you want to show up in a three-piece suit? or
- Do you want to show up business casual, with a bit of flair and class?

I spent fifteen years in finance. During those first ten years in Chicago, it was a very formal business, and you were expected to attend meetings and events in suits or slacks and suit jackets.

When I moved to San Diego, our clients came to meetings in Tommy Bahama shorts and silk shirts with their flip flops. When I moved into fitness, I pretty much LIVED in Lululemon and other high-end fitness apparel. What I found after a few years of that is I was tired of always looking like I didn't put any effort into how I looked! I dressed in top of the line fitness apparel, but I normally had my hair up in a ponytail and skipped the make up! I was wearing leggings, bulky sweaters, and ballet flats, and I always looked and felt frumpy!

It had gotten so bad that once, I put on a pair of jeans and some make up and my husband walked in and asked where we were going because he was so used to me never putting any effort into my looks! As I have transitioned back into business, I have adopted a style that is a bit more my own. I have now gone back to a more laid back, casual, but polished look. If I'm not teaching or taking a fitness class, I now go into the studio in nice shorts, cute shoes, and a cute little top. If I'm going to a networking event, I wear a fabulous pair of skinny jeans with some awesome heels and a cute button up top and jewelry!

If I'm doing something fun or social, you'll often find me in leather high-heeled booties, skinny jeans, and a jacket (often leather) - still not cutting edge, but certainly more sharp and unique than before! I recently went to a national women's conference, and I was amazed at the difference in how everyone was dressed. We had women dressed:

- To the nines in designer dresses
- In shorts and flip flops
- In fitness apparel
- In baggy casual wear

All were acceptable in the environment, but each outfit presented the person and their business and personality before the person ever said a word. If you are serious about your new business, you definitely need to make a very concerted decision about how you want to show up. How do you want people to see you and remember you?

If you're trying to be known as a fitness expert, showing up in top notch fitness apparel is totally appropriate.

If you are trying to work in the luxury market, you better show up epitomizing luxury.

Whatever you are, be a good one.
Abraham Lincoln

If your market is about getting AWAY from the stuffiness of corporate America, you probably don't want to be wearing a suit, stockings, and heels. For example, if you are building an online business that is based on freeing your clients from the shackles of corporate America, then don't show up like you would to a corporate event! This is when you will likely want an amazing designer dress or sun dress with a fabulous sweater and/or amazing strappy sandals.

If you are serious about putting your best foot forward, I strongly suggest you consider meeting with a Personal Stylist or a Personal Branding Expert.

Stop wearing your wishbone
where your backbone out to be.
Elizabeth Gilbert

As I mentioned above, last year, I hired a Personal Branding Expert (Kelly Lucente) to help me make sense of my own personal brand. I had spent 15 years in corporate America. Then I spent five years in fitness. I was making a transition back to a business setting, but a business setting that involved working on my computer from a luxury resort – not sitting in meetings all day, every day! I was having a hard time making the adjustment about what my style and brand would look like.

Kelly and I went through my plans for my business:

- Who would I be working with? (Who was my target client?)
- What was their problem I would be solving?
- How would I be solving it?
- Would I be doing only online work?
- Would I be hitting a speaking circuit?
- Was I trying to get media attention?
- Would I be doing networking events?
- What did I want to portray on my website? Would I be working with corporations?

Each of these things were important to determine how I "showed up." Ultimately, we identified that my target client was women who either were in corporate America and wanted to leave, or women who were business consultants who wanted to stop trading dollars for hours and wanted to build a business that used more of their intellectual property and less of their hours!

These women wanted more freedom. They wanted to trade in their suit for jeans or designer dresses! They wanted to be able to take their computer to a five-star hotel and work by the pool with their umbrella drink. So, my wardrobe changed. My website images changed. We did photo shoots that portrayed the lifestyle I loved and others aspired to, with a fusion of images of me on a couch in ripped jeans, a sweater and my computer. We also created images of me with a beach hat, a glass of wine, and my computer, with the ocean in the background. My purpose is that I wanted to illustrate that I work, and I work hard. Because I am self-employed, doesn't mean my life is easy. It just means that I have more freedoms and flexibilities about how and when I work!

When I go to a networking event, I want to be one of the most well-dressed women in the room - where before, I always wanted to fit in. I decided that with my new branding, I wanted to stand out! So, I have leveled up my wardrobe and am trading in my ballet flats for killer heels and an amazing jacket in leathers, creams, burgundies, royal blues, and other strong, classic colors.

Do the Work:

Who is your target client?

_____

_____

_____

What are their pain points?

_____

_____

_____

What are their dreams/aspirations?

_____

_____

_____

How do you need to show up to be motivational to them?

_____

_____

_____

What message do you want your wardrobe to portray?

_____

_____

_____

What message do you want your website to portray?

_____

_____

_____

What type of imagery do you want on your website to speak to them?

_____

_____

_____

Is your goal to be a public speaker?

_____

_____

_____

Will you be attending networking events?

_____

_____

_____

How will those around you show up to these events?

_____

_____

_____

How will you stand out in these events?

_____

_____

_____

Are you attempting to get media coverage?

_____

_____

_____

How do you want to show up in media?

_____

_____

_____

Will you be working with corporations?

_____

_____

_____

How will you show up?

_____

_____

_____

I have covered some of the basics of your personal style, but I strongly suggest that anyone that wants to build a top notch business considers consulting with an image consultant or personal branding professional. Between what I spent on clothes I don't use, photographs that didn't represent my brand direction, and multiple website redo's, I strongly suggest you consult a personal branding expert. Here are a few of my favorites:

Branding Resources:

- Personal Styling – JuliannStitick.com
- Business and Personal Branding – KellyLucente.com

Business Etiquette and How You Are Viewed in a Professional Environment:

As you are trying to determine how you are going to show up, let's consider a few of the common issues that you will face that will affect how you are seen in social situations.

Manners Still Matter

Have you ever been at an event and found someone to be completely boorish? They interrupt conversations, have to be the center of attention, speak over others, smack their food, or tell jokes that are completely inappropriate for the setting?

I'm guessing that at some point you have been at an event with this person. (Maybe you've even been this person.) You can be the best dressed, most well-put, together person in a room, and if you open your mouth and look like a complete idiot, your chances of winning business have likely just gone out the door!

Here are some of your business etiquette basics:

Make Introductions

Have you ever entered a party conversation and you know only one person in the conversation, and they make no effort to introduce you, or maybe you are attending a social event with your husband, and don't know any of the other guests? If you're a bit introverted like me, it is a very uncomfortable place to be. When someone will take the time to make an introduction to someone else, it really helps take the pressure off.

When you're in a professional setting (or even a social setting) and someone new joins the conversation, attempt to make all the introductions you can. Introduce the participants by name, and ideally, say something positive about them to break the ice. For example, if my husband walked up, I would say something like this to Mrs. Mary Smith, "Mary, I would like to introduce you to my husband, Mike. Mike is a real estate consultant in Carlsbad, California, and we've been married for 15 years. Mike, this is Mary Smith. Mary runs an art gallery in Rancho Santa Fe, California. We met at a networking event a few years ago. She has some beautiful pieces in her gallery that may be a great fit for your clients." By making the introduction and trying to find something that these two people have in common, it makes it much simpler for them to pick up the conversation successfully!

Also, people LIKE connectors! One of the best things about my husband, Mike, and I going to events together is that I remember things about people and Mike always seems to know everyone, and is not afraid to speak to anyone in the room! Together we make great connectors, and shine in introducing people that we believe should know each other based on their business needs or personal interests!

A great way for people to remember you fondly is if you have taken the time to get to know them and connected them with someone else that may be able to help them grow their business!

No need to hurry. No need to sparkle.
No need to be anybody but oneself.
Virginia Woolf

Personal Space and a Handshake Are Still Professional Courtesies

When you are meeting someone new, a handshake is a professional and respectful way to introduce yourself. A nod or a hello may be more typical than it had been in the past, but the way to set yourself apart from the crowd is to do the right thing - not necessarily the typical thing. For example, if you are sitting at a table and someone new comes up to sit next to you, the most professional thing that you can do is stand up, look them in the eye, introduce yourself, and shake hands. This shows a level of respect both for your new guest as well as yourself.

In a social or a business setting, be cautious about becoming TOO familiar. I don't know about you, but I'm not a hugger! I hug my closest friends and my family, but I don't hug strangers, and I don't like to be hugged BY strangers! Do you remember that scene in Dirty Dancing when Patrick Swayze put his arms out in a semi-circle and said to Jennifer Grey, "This is my dance space. THIS is your dance space."? That's how I feel about my personal space. I don't want people nose to nose with me in a conversation, and I don't want to walk into a large networking event and have people hugging me.

Always look around. Know your surroundings, and be courteous of others' personal space. If someone is speaking to you and you notice that they are trying to back away, don't keep moving closer to them. They are likely trying to create more personal space.

All we have is all we need. All we need is the
awareness of how blessed we really are.
Sarah Ban Breathnach

Pay Attention

Our society has this horrible habit of not listening and interrupting people! They say that God gave us two ears and one mouth for a reason. Despite the fact that we should listen half as much as we talk, we always seem to be ready to say our next thing or make our next point. Often, we are so busy thinking of what we are going to say next that we aren't even listening to what those around us are saying.

To truly make someone feel like they are being heard, take the time to listen to them. Nod as they speak. Look them in the eye. Don't be looking over their head for the next person that you'll be speaking to - and for goodness' sake, put your phone away! Take the time to truly hear those around you!

Have you ever been at a dinner table and every single person at the table is on their phone? A few years ago, my brother and sister-in-law were moving from San Diego to Nashville. The four of us (my brother Chad, sister-in-law Julie, husband Mike, and I) decided to go out to dinner the night before they left. They were literally moving across the country, but there the four of us were, sitting in an amazing restaurant all posting on Facebook and seeing what was happening on our phones.

Sometimes we are so self-absorbed that we miss what is going on around us! Take a few moments and pay attention to those around you! If you're hanging out with the right people, you'll rarely be sorry!

Watch What You Say and How You Say It

We all know the girl that drops F bombs throughout a conversation and tells jokes that are completely inappropriate! That girl is NOT representing herself in the best possible way. I have seen just a couple of women that are completely able to pull off being a bit crude or crass and it seems to be their true and authentic personality, but it is definitely the exception versus the rule. Even if it is their authentic personality, that doesn't mean it isn't offensive to those around them. In my fitness studio, we have had instructors that use words that just aren't appropriate. As the business owner, I will often get emails from clients saying that they won't take a certain class again because they were offended by what an instructor said. Fortunately, these clients have often told me when these situations arise. However, how many other clients may I have lost due to the client that won't tell me when they were offended by someone's actions? You just never know what someone is thinking. Be cautious about the words you use and the image you portray.

I know a few business owners who drop F bombs and say colorful things all the time. They ARE aware of it. And they feel like that is who they are and that they aren't for everyone. If that is a decision you choose to make, that is fine. Just know that If you ARE going to use words, language, or images that some may find offensive, make sure that you are making this decision consciously and understand that you will attract a certain person to your tribe, while potentially repelling others!

Also, be careful about speaking about other people, or alienating people with divisive subjects. I tell my husband, Mike, to use his filter - and you always know when he doesn't and he says something that you know is just completely inappropriate!

I'm not saying that you have to censor everything you say and avoid being yourself. I am just saying that if you are genuinely concerned about how you show up in this world, consider thinking before you speak, and make sure that what you mean is what you are saying!

Be Punctual

I am originally from the Midwest. When we set an appointment for 3 pm, we are normally there at 2:55. If we find that we are going to be even just a couple of minutes late, we call and let the other person know. When I moved to San Diego at age 24, I was shocked by how few people arrive anywhere on time. If church starts at 11 am, the pews are often empty until about 11:20. If people are attending a dinner that is supposed to be served at 6:30, it is not uncommon that many attendees aren't even arriving until 7 pm.

In my opinion, there is no quicker way to tell someone that they are unimportant than to arrive to a meeting or event with them late and not let them know. Whether it is your intention or not, by showing up late, you are telling them that your time was more important than theirs and that it was not important to you to be on time for them.

You may be trying to get "just one more thing" done, but if it is going to make you late for a scheduled appointment with someone else, don't do it! Be on time. Show those around you that they and their time matter to you! You may be amazed at how differently they see you!

Dining Out

Have you ever gone to a restaurant for a business event and not known how to behave? What fork to use, what to order, etc? I always think of Julia Roberts in *Pretty Woman* looking at the escargots trying to determine how to eat them, and then sending one flying across the room. It is one of those iconic moments where I could totally imagine myself in a situation like that, making myself look silly and uninformed!

Unfortunately, I believe that our schools are missing the boat in not providing education on some simple life skills. I believe that basic business etiquette is one of the things that we should be taught in high school! We're not going to get into all elements of etiquette, but I do want to cover the big things that will affect how you are seen in a professional business setting.

Ordering Your Food

Lady and The Tramp is an adorable movie. Who doesn't love watching these two sweet animals each slurp their spaghetti? However, what was adorable for these two animated animals isn't adorable for you or for me! So, here's the first and simplest tip - think it through. If you think it may be messy and will be hard to eat in front of people, maybe you shouldn't order it in a business setting!

A couple of no no's in my book are:

- Ribs - If you have tons of barbecue sauce and need to use your fingers to pick them up, it's just a bad idea. A good rule of thumb: if they are going to give you a bib with your dinner, you probably don't want to order that!
- Chicken wings – Just like the ribs, if they are finger-licking good (and you're likely to lick your fingers to clean it up), then there is likely a better dinner option!
- Spaghetti – Just TRY rolling the spaghetti around your fork and not slurping it up into your mouth. It's much easier said than done!
- Crab/Lobster (cracking it, pulling it apart, etc). Much like the chicken wings and ribs, these two items can be very messy. If

you need to use your fingers to crack your crab or lobster, there may be a better choice!

- Corn on the cob – Stuff in between your teeth is NEVER good in the middle of a business dinner!
- Ordering five courses and alcohol when everyone else is ordering salads or a single course - no one likes to pay the bill for the one person who is just looking at an event as a free, unlimited meal.

The simplest rule of thumb is that if it may embarrass you, skip it. If it detracts from your ability to participate in the meeting or event, skip it. If it may make you look rude, inappreciative, or greedy, skip it!

Silverware

The easiest way to get through a formal business dinner in your silverware is to work from the outside in. The furthest fork on the left is normally your appetizer or salad fork (whatever their first course is). As you get closer to your plate, you normally get a new utensil with each and every course.

Another simple guide is that if it is on the left, it is likely a fork and goes with four letters, much like food. The things on the right of your plate are your glasses, your bread plates, etc. It's a simple way to remember which plate, glass or soup bowl is yours!

Who Picks Up the Check?

So this should be simple: the person that makes the invite is the host. The host is responsible for the bill. If you invite someone to dinner, then you are responsible for the check. If there is a dispute, don't ever fight over it, but make the effort to pay the check!

If it's a large group dinner, it may be safe to assume that the bill will be split among all the participants. Have you ever gone out to dinner with a group of friends or business associates and one person just keeps ordering and ordering?

I attended a conference last year and a group of four of us went to dinner after the day of meetings. Three of us ordered a single cocktail and a single entrée. One person ordered an appetizer, three cocktails, an entrée, and dessert. While I would normally be just fine splitting the bill, this was just not appropriate behavior. Two of us went to the server offline and asked for separate checks for the entire party. At the end of dinner, the single diner said, "So we'll just split the bill, right?" He was pretty surprised to find that the server had already split all our checks and he was responsible for his entire bill – almost $200 vs. about $40 for each of the rest of us. I don't know that our handling was in line with Emily Post, but I am pretty certain that we did what was right. I'm also hoping that our dining companion remembers this experience next time he wants to make the assumption that everyone will pay for his exorbitant meal!

---

*It's not the situation, but whether we react
(negative) or respond (positive) to the situation
that's important.*
Zig Ziglar

Networking

I want to take a moment to debunk a popular myth. Many people think that if they start going to networking events that they are going to have tons of business. I had been active in a networking group, and I was amazed by the comments that said something like this, "Yes, I went once, but I didn't get any business from it so I never went back."

Maybe you see the networking event as the opportunity to go schedule private coffees with everyone you meet. (I don't necessarily advocate that either). One of the reasons I stopped networking for a couple of years was that every event I went to, people were asking me to a private coffee, and they were trying to sell me on their products.

I recently was speaking with a founder of a successful San Diego networking group. I was amazed by how often people expect to just show up for an event and have a line at their business door. I was also amazed at how many people saw a networking event as an opportunity to go collect business cards and just add people to their database.

On my business card I use an email address that is super clean and that I use to correspond solely with clients. I don't give that email address to vendors. I don't even give that email address to most of my family or friends. So if I start getting unsolicited emails on that email address, I consider them to be spam.

If we meet at a networking event and someone wants to add me to their list, all they need to do is email me and ask my permission. I will then give them my email address where I receive other emails and all my subscriptions. I am often willing and happy to get these emails. I just don't want to meet someone, give them my business card, and then end up getting pitched their goods and services every day.

The guidelines for success in networking are simple. Networking is the practice of building good, long-term, symbiotic business relationships that are built on sharing knowledge, resources, and referrals. It is not the collection of business cards. It is not the scheduling of coffees to try to get someone to buy your services.

Now, I'm not saying don't schedule coffee! One of the best ways to build these networking relationships is to do one-on-one or small group events, but don't view these events as an opportunity to sell your services without first establishing the relationships!

Remember also that networking is about connecting! After a networking event, go find your new connections on LinkedIn and connect there. Send them a personal message about how much you enjoyed meeting them. Schedule a follow-up meeting by phone, FaceTime, Skype, or in person. Go with an agenda to find out what you can do to help them. If you unselfishly try to help them, then you will likely find that they are willing to open their rolodex to see how they can help you too!

When you are at networking events, look for ways to help those you meet. Look for ways to connect your new friends to others that may be able to help! Human beings are interesting creatures. When someone helps us, we often want to reciprocate! It's one of the best ways to build your business! Give to others! You'll be surprised how much comes back to you!

The difference between a wise and foolish
man is this – the former sees much, thinks much,
and speaks little; but the latter speaks more than
he either sees or thinks.
William Scott Downey, Proverbs

Social Media

Your digital footprint is big and long reaching. Whenever I get a resume from a prospective staff member, I immediately check their social media channels to determine how they portray themselves in the world. If their social media is full of fish-lipped selfies, they may not be the person I want dealing with luxury corporations.

If there are pictures of them inebriated all over town, that doesn't provide me with oodles of confidence either! Are they going to show up to work on time? Are they going to drunkenly blab secrets all over town? If they are a representative of the company, how will they be perceived?

Remember that when you are posting something online, it is likely leaving an impression. This is not the place to be rude, condescending, or fight with others over religion or politics. I have already told you that my husband, Mike, is a complete open book. Well, occasionally he posts things about both him and I that I don't believe are in alignment with our personal brands. The other day he posted a photo of me in my pjs, glasses and bed head. Then the next day he posted a photo standing on a scale with his weight and gross feet. I'm all for authentic, but not flat out scary!

Remember, even if you believe that your photos are private, somehow it seems that most can still be seen! EVERY single thing that you do, you need to consider what message it is sending and who will potentially receive the message!

You can tell more about a person by
what he says about others
than you can by what others say about him.
Audrey Hepburn

CHAPTER 5:
Your Business Plan

If plan A fails, remember there are
25 more letters.
Chris Guillebeau

I am always shocked when I meet a business owner who is experiencing difficulties in their business, and when I ask them about their business plan, they look at me blankly. "Business plan?" they say… "Why do I need a business plan? I didn't need to get financing for my business. There was no point in wasting time on a business plan."

I always liken it to Steven Covey's example of climbing the corporate ladder, only to realize when you got to the top that it was leaning against the wrong wall the entire time. If you are building a business and you don't have a specific plan for it, how will you identify whether or not a business opportunity is the right fit or another "shiny object?"

As an entrepreneur, one of the biggest challenges that I face is that I have so many "great" ideas that I always want to do all of them. I call this my "shiny object syndrome" - and no, I didn't coin the phrase, and it's not unique to me. It is a "syndrome" that I believe probably 95% of all true entrepreneurs face. I will get into some of the big uses of your business plan in just a moment, but ultimately, I want you to get this main point:

You need to look at your business plan as your ROADMAP! It will be your living, breathing, ever-changing plan that details the DIRECTION of your business.

Without continual growth and progress, such words as improvement, achievement, and success have no meaning.
Benjamin Franklin.

Your business plan will change as you grow and change, but I like to always remind my clients that they don't want to be changing their business plan on a daily basis, based on their whims. Your business plan should be the measuring stick of whether or not something fits into your business, not a document to be changed every time an opportunity arises.

Your business plan serves a number of different purposes:

- If you ever need financing, a lender will require a business plan to evaluate the strength of your business concept. This business plan will normally require financial projections as part of the business plan.
- If you ever want to rent space for the business, the landlord will normally require a business plan and financials. This business plan will normally require financial projections as part of the business plan.
- Your business plan will be your opportunity to really delve into your target client and who you are going to serve – giving you clarity on all future branding, marketing, and services.

- Your business plan gives you a format for identifying dangers, opportunities, strengths, weaknesses, and threats, and planning ahead for these in your business.
- Your business plan will allow you to identify or disqualify marketing opportunities based on your target client.
- Your business plan will help you determine if it is financially viable or appropriate to add a new product or service to your existing core business.
- Your business plan may include a potential exit strategy to help you determine at what point in the business you will consider selling or closing the business.

So, now that you know what you will do with your business plan, let's identify what you want to put in your business plan.

*Do not go where the path may lead, go
instead where there is no path and leave a trail.*
Ralph Waldo Emerson

Elements of a Great Business Plan that will guide you in the growth of your business:

- Name of the Company
- Ownership of the Company/Legal – will there be a legal entity that holds the business? – See Legal Chapter
- Information on the Business and Owner (This is most important if you are renting space or need to get financing.)
- Description of Your Product or Service
- History of the Company
- Will there be office space required, rental space required, etc.?

- Personnel and Management – Who will you be hiring to do what tasks?
- Economics of the Business – How will you fund the business? See Finance Chapter
- Market Analysis
    - Target Client
    - Key Competitors
    - Strengths
    - Weaknesses
    - Opportunities
    - Threats
- Marketing Plan – See Marketing Chapter
- Marketing Schedule – See Marketing Chapter

Business Plan – The Basics

The beginning of your business plan should be simple. You start with the name of the company and the ownership of the company (is there a legal entity that owns the business?).

What is the name of your company?

_____

_____

How will your company be owned?
(You may need to read the Legal Chapter to know more about this.)

_____

_____

Tell me about the business.

Do you need to get financing? If so, how much? Do you have capital to bring to the table in addition to any financing? How would you anticipate getting financing (credit cards, home equity line, small business loan)?

_____

_____

_____

Will you be renting space? If so, tell me about it? How much square footage? How will you use the space? Do you need certain rooms built out? Do you need bathrooms, or other expensive things built into the space?

_____

_____

_____

Tell me about you as the owner and your business background (educational experience, business experience, years in business, skills that make you ready to open, build, and run this business).

_____

_____

_____

Tell me about the history of this company.
- Is it a franchise?
- Is it a family business that you are taking over and taking in a different direction?
  How did the business come about?

_____

_____

_____

Tell me about the anticipated start-up costs. Include equipment, rent, payroll, insurance, etc. See the Finance Chapter for Specifics to include in this.

_____

_____

_____

Tell me about your staffing and anticipated team.

- When you launch the business, will it be just you?
- Will you have a staff right away?
- Will you launch the business then have a manager take over the daily management of the business?

_____

_____

_____

Do you need to take a salary from the business right away, or can you afford to wait?

_____

_____

_____

How long will it take for the revenues of the business to pay for the expenses of the business?

_____

_____

_____

How long will it take for the revenues of the business to be able to pay back anticipated loans and/or to pay you as the owner?

_____

_____

_____

It's so great to find that one special person
you want to annoy for the rest of your life.
Rita Rudner

Business Plan – Identifying Your Target Client

The first (and in my opinion, most important) element of your business plan is Identifying Your Target Client. Your target client will be the one person that all your products and services are built for. They are the person that you have imagined in your business as your best client and the clients you want to attract for your business.

Just to be clear – you will have OTHER types of clients too, but your ideal client is the SINGLE person that you are building your services for! Imagine if you were to go to work every day and you were serving your favorite person ever. Who would that person be? What qualities and traits do they have?

One of the biggest things for you to identify before you open any type of business is WHO IS YOUR TARGET CLIENT?

- What is his/her gender? (For this analysis, I'm going to assume a female.)

- What is her age group?

- Is she married?

- Does she have kids?

- Where does she live?

- Does she own or rent her home?

- Where does she shop?

- What clothes does she wear?

- Where would you find her spending her time on a weekend?

- Where does she vacation?

- What brands is she passionate about?

- What publications does she read? (magazines, news, websites, blogs)

- What are her interests?

- What is her health/fitness level?

- What DRIVES your target client?

Now that you have answered these questions, I want to ask you to write a story about it.

Practical Application: Who's Your Target Client?

In my barre studio, I have TWO ideal clients! All marketing is designed for each of them. They are very similar in many ways, but have a few distinct differences that play into our schedule and class creation.

Ideal Client – Mommy Melanie

For our morning classes, my ideal client is Mommy Melanie. She is between 30 and 40 years old and is a stay-at-home mom who wants to stay in shape but only has so much time. She needs her work out to be quick and efficient. She loves running into the other mommies that she knows from her daughter's school. We have designed the morning schedule to work around her busy life and the school drop off schedule. Our classes were designed to incorporate cardio and resistance in an hour or less. She can come in and get a full-body workout. We offer coffee for our 12-month members because we know that Mommy Melanie is busy and needs to get everything done quickly! She comes in to class with the most recent Lululemon and Apple products, and maybe stopped by the Starbucks drive thru for her latte on the way in. On Saturday you would find her at the local spa getting a massage and a manicure!

In life there is always that special person who shapes who you are, who helps to determine the person you become.
Molly Ringwald

Ideal client – Corporate Carissa

Our second ideal client is named Corporate Carissa. Carissa is between the ages of 25 and 45. She is a busy, professional woman who likely works 8-5. She works within about 3-5 miles of the studio, and she is health and fitness minded. She is busy and often feels like her time comes last. She enjoys spending time with her friends and family but knows she needs to take care of herself and needs her work out to be convenient to her life. She may come to class at 6 am, run in for an express class on her lunch break at noon, or come by after work, before she goes home at the end of the day. She is another busy woman, and her class formats and class times have been designed for her to be able to get out of work, get to the studio, and change clothes before class starts.

In the studio, I go back to these two personas before I make ANY changes to the business model of the studio. If I am going to add a new type of class, I need to feel confident that the class offering is going to supplement our existing offerings and will be a fit for our clients. In the same way, before I bring in new retail apparel, candles, jewelry, scarves, etc., I want to believe with a fair amount of certainty that it is the right fit for our clientele.

In my consulting business, I work with women who often started in corporate America and want to have a career with more flexibility and freedom. On this side of my business, I have three different client personas. Each is very different, and there is a different product or service for each and every one of them. Before I waste the time creating a new product or service, I run the product/service through my client persona. Is it a fit?

Once you know the ideal client, you now need to answer some other questions... Why do they need you? What can you offer your client to improve their life?

Why You?

- What problem does your target client have that you will solve?

- How will you solve it?

- What can your target client afford to solve the problem?

- Will it save them money?

- Will it make them money?

- Will it make them healthier, happier?

- Will it give them more freedom?

- What is that worth to them?

Once you identify these answers, you will be better able to determine the pricing for your product or service!

BE specific!

If you're dealing with a fitness client, don't say that she wants to lose weight! Don't say that she wants to work out!

One of my driving forces is that my studio clients are busy women who are craving true community, want to make personal connections, and need their work out to be fast, effective and efficient. They need to get both cardio and muscle sculpting as quickly as possible. Therefore, every class and activity we create in the studio is based on these objectives! Every single class offers a total-body workout and incorporates both cardio and resistance in a 60 minute (or less) class.

Because they also crave community, we often create classes specifically for our best members. These classes are Member Only and it creates exclusivity to the classes. It also allows these classes to be a bit smaller and for the clients to get to know each other better. One of the other things we do is to incorporate partner exercises or social times to encourage these clients to become friends and support each other. Eventually these clients will check in on each other and schedule their classes around getting together! It is amazing how much more loyal a client is when they feel like they matter – to the business and the other clients that they see on a regular basis.

With my consulting business, the filter is simple – will it help a woman be more efficient, have more freedom and/or make more money, while doing something they enjoy? If it doesn't meet those objectives for my clients, it doesn't deserve the time or energy from me!

Do The Work.

Ok, now that we've gone through what is included in your target client, I want you to actually do the work.

Please name and describe your target client:

_____

_____

_____

Now that you have the who, what and WHY of your client, I want you to complete this exercise.

PLEASE don't skip this. I know it sounds corny, but all future marketing needs to be written as if you are speaking to THIS ONE PERSON – NOT THE MASSES!

Please describe this person and tell me a story about her (or him). Name her. What is her name? What is her age? Where does she work? Where does she shop? WHY?

_____

_____

_____

Once you have this entire description, please take some time and really think on this person. Now, when you write your website, your social media posts, your flyers, brochures, welcome emails and everything else, you will speak to that one person.

One common mistake in marketing is to speak to the population as a whole. Have you ever opened an email that says, "Hi everyone. I want to make an offer." I don't know about you, but I take that email very differently than I would an email that says, "Hi Amy, I have JUST the RIGHT thing that will solve YOUR problem!"

What is your mission?

Next in your business plan, you need to have a Mission Statement. Again, write this as if you are speaking to ONE person!

What is the true goal and purpose of YOUR business?

_____

_____

_____

Your mission statement should include three things:

Who do you serve?

_____

_____

_____

What do you offer them?

_____

_____

_____

Why should they choose you?

_____

_____

_____

Again, be specific and speak to your one target client. As a business consultant, my mission is simple: Everything in my business is designed to help women who are tired, frustrated, and burnt out in their current business life find a better way to run their life and their business to have more time, money, and freedom for the things that matter most to them.

I'm a workaholic! I feel most comfortable when I'm working. Even when I go on vacation, I am reading business books and learning. Freedom to me is the ability to do what I want, when I want, from a location that suits me. So my products and services are all designed to help women have that same experience in their lives.

Do The Work:

What is the mission of your business?

_____

_____

_____

You have competition every day because you set such high standards for yourself that you have to go out every day and live up to that.
Michael Jordan

Who is your competition?

When I am consulting with potential fitness studio owners, one of the first questions I get is about competition. Is competition helpful to the launch of your business, or is competition harmful? Ultimately, I think that it all depends.

If you have done the work in:

- Identifying your target client
- Writing the best mission statement, you can
- Creating a unique product/service that meets the needs of your target client
- Delivering value beyond your competition

If you have excelled in these areas of your business, competition is probably good. Competition will help shoulder some of the time, expense, and burden of educating your market. However, if you are cutting corners, riding on someone else's coat tails, not providing a unique experience and trying to be like everyone else, competition is probably bad. There is nothing to set you apart from everyone else in the market place. So when clients are looking for a person who provides your service, they will choose based exclusively on location or price – making you a commodity that really has no value. The only way to ever compete in this scenario is to be the low-cost provider (which is not ideal).

When I opened my first barre studio, there were only three other studios in the entire COUNTY of San Diego! That is not many studios for such a large city/county. I was offering a very unique type of fitness. In addition, I was also offering a unique type of barre. At that time, every other studio focused solely on muscle sculpting, and my studio offered sculpting and cardio, all in one workout. I had the opportunity to get a large market share quickly because there was no competition.

However, because there was no competition, I was also forced to spend time, money, and resources to educate the market on my offerings and services! When I first started, every time I said I had a barre studio, I was met with a blank stare followed by a question about alcohol!

Now, over five years later, there are over 30 studios in the county! That is quite a bit of competition – and not necessarily good!

If you have done the work described in the past few tips, you can set yourself apart so hopefully you can stay head of the competition. If you look like everyone else, however, then the competition will be harmful to you, and nothing will encourage clients to choose you over the low cost provider.

Competition is the keen cutting edge of business,
always shaving away at costs.
Henry Ford

Do The Work:

Identify Your Competitors:

Please list ALL competition within your space.

_____

_____

_____

Who are they?

_____

_____

_____

What do they offer?

_____

_____

_____

How does it compare to your offerings?

_____

_____

_____

What is their pricing structure?

_____

_____

_____

How does it compare?

_____

_____

_____

What do people love about them?

_____

_____

_____

What do people hate about them?

_____

_____

_____

Once you have this list, we will be doing a Strengths, Weaknesses, Opportunities, Threats (SWOT) analysis. This will allow you to identify your competitors and set yourself apart.

Strength does not come from winning. Your struggles develop your strengths. When you go through hardships and decide not to surrender, that is strength.
Arnold Schwarzenegger

Your Strengths

Now that you have your list of competitors, I want you to create a list of YOUR strengths vs. your competitors.

- It may be that you plan on being a VERY involved owner that will provide in-person leadership and personality. (People do business with those that they know, like and trust.)
- It may be that you have a "secret weapon" that you think will be critical to the success of your business.
- It may be who you plan to hire.
- It may be how you plan to deliver your services.
- It may be that you are offering a new, unique service that will allow you to be first to market, capturing large market share.
- It may be that you have figured out how to deliver a high-value service for a lower cost.
- Are you good with technology and automation?
- Are you a natural-born sales person?

Do The Work:

List ALL your potential strengths and compare them to your competitor.

_____

_____

_____

*Success is achieved by developing our
strengths, not by eliminating our weaknesses.
Marilyn vos Savant*

Your Weaknesses

Now that you have your list of competitors and your strengths,
I want you to do exactly the same thing for weaknesses.

- What do you feel you may not do well?
- What do you see that someone else does really well that you
  may not measure up to?
- This could be culture.
- This could be about you.
- This could be about a potential staff member.
- This could be that someone else has tons of money to throw
  at their business and you don't.
- Do you have no business experience?
- Do you have no support?

For me, one of my HUGE weaknesses is staffing. I am NOT a
natural leader of staff. I am impatient. I am easily annoyed. I am
a lifelong learner. I don't want someone on my staff that isn't
willing to learn and grow, and I don't like to hear excuses from a
staff member for why something isn't being done.

I quickly learned that I needed some help in the staffing part of
my business. I needed a manager to insulate the staff from me
(and me from them). I needed a sales coach to help come in and
teach the team to sell. Then I learned that one of the best ways to
automate the training of my staff was to create an online portal
with video training taught by me. This way when my staff person

said that they weren't trained on something, I could point to the video that they were told to watch in their first day with our company.

Life is very interesting... in the end, some of your greatest pains become your greatest strengths.
Drew Barrymore

Do The Work

List your weaknesses and compare them to your competitors. What do you feel that you don't/won't do well? Once you know what you don't do well, you can identify ways to either improve it or work around it.

Opportunity is missed by most people because it is dressed in overalls and looks like work.
Thomas Edison

List Your Opportunities

Your opportunities are all the things you see about your competitors' weaknesses that you think you can do better. For example, does their product or service need improvement that you feel you can provide?

- Do they have room for improvement in their staff?

- Do they have enough activities to build community, or can you do that better?

- What do you see as opportunities for you to make your business better than their business?

A pessimist sees the difficulty in every opportunity; an optimist sees the opportunity in every difficulty.
Winston Churchill

Homework:

List your opportunities – the things you can do better than your competitors.

_____

_____

_____

When did the future switch from being a
promise
to being a threat?
Unknown

List Your Threats

- What are the things that will threaten your success?

  Is your business idea a trend?

- Are you envisioning a ton of competition that isn't there right now?

-
  Will you be operating on a shoestring budget? (In particular, if unanticipated expenses or challenges arise, will you have the capital to move past them?)

- Do you have/or not have the support of your family and friends?

- Will you be doing all the work by yourself, leading to potential burn out?

- Are you afraid of technology - meaning that it will be harder and longer for you to potentially build your business? (or maybe that you have to work harder to build your business because you can't automate with technology and automation)

Threats don't work with the person who's got
nothing to lose.
Maduro Ash

Homework:

List the things that threaten the potential success of your business. The sooner you know them, the better you can potentially work around them!

_____

_____

_____

Getting a Business Loan

Not all business launches need a business loan. I opened my first business without a business loan. When I opened my second, however, I did need a business loan. If you are hoping to get a business loan, there are a number of things that you need to do to increase your chances.

1) Your credit needs to be good – likely 700 or more.
2) Have a completed Balance Sheet – See attached resources
3) Have a completed Income/Expense Statement – See attached resources
4) You need to have a solid business plan. Use the resources we are providing to get started. A lender wants to know

that you know what you are doing and that you have a plan and ability to repay their loan.

Potential loan resources:

1) Your personal bank or credit union
2) Your local Small Business Association
3) Your local SCORE office
4) Your retirement plan (you are paying back yourself)

Your next items that you will need in your business plan will be a marketing plan and a marketing schedule. The Marketing Chapter has more information on building a marketing plan for your business.

An investment in knowledge pays the best interest.
Benjamin Franklin.

CHAPTER 6
Protecting Your Assets

---

*It's not how much you make, but how much
money you keep, how hard it works for you, and
how many generations you keep it for.*
Robert Kiyosaki

We all hate it, but it must be done. As a new business owner, you will likely be amazed by all the legal obligations you must meet over the course of a year. I often meet business owners who try to skip the legal steps. Unfortunately, what most who operate this way don't understand is that there may be some things that will never cause a problem, but there may be some legal steps skipped that may come back to totally bite them in the tush – sometimes in a very expensive way...

Your initial legal requirements may include:

- Your legal entity/tax id number
- Your state sales tax
- Your city/county business license
- Building permits
- Occupancy/use permits
- Unemployment Insurance
- Worker's Comp Insurance
- Liability Insurance

Your legal entity is a big decision. We will cover this in depth later this chapter. But ultimately, I need you to know this... If you are starting a type of business that has any type of liability, then you need an entity to protect yourself and your family from potential lawsuits, expenses, etc.

Your Tax ID Number is the number that your business will report to both the IRS and the state about income taxes for your business. You will need this number when you apply for permits, business licenses, employee accounts, bank accounts, and more! Do this EARLY in the process! If you wait, you will have to go back and unwind a lot of your legal work later!

Business Licenses are required based on the type of business, your state, and your city. It is strongly encouraged that you contact your attorney and verify any type of licenses you will need to operate your business and meet all your legal obligations. For most cities, you are required to set up a fictitious business name (doing business as name) and file for a business license. This business license normally includes a nominal fee to the city and/or county and an annual reporting or fee requirement.

Permits. Depending on your type of business, permits may or may not be required. Every city, county, and state has different requirements for licenses and permits. You may want to research various cities before deciding where you will be building your business. Some cities have significantly more stringent requirements than other cities.

Practical Application

Last weekend I was sitting with a studio owner in Northern California. She has run into more legal and permitting challenges than any other studio owner I have ever worked with. The city has required a number of bathrooms, water fountains, parking studies, and an architect before they would approve her location.

However, while I was there, we visited another new studio that was only about two miles away from her new studio. As we were in the new studio, I asked her why they didn't have the same "features" that she was being required to put in her studio. The simple answer, despite the fact that they were only two miles apart, one was in one city and one was in another – with her city having much more stringent requirements!

The lesson in this, know some of these license requirements, permitting, requirements, and other legal obligations BEFORE you choose your location! Had she known all these things before she decided on her location, she likely would have chosen something different!

Some of the things that you could be required to have permits for:
- Building/Construction
- Zoning of your type of business
- Parking
- Food/alcohol
- Services provided
- Health department permits
- Fire and police permits
- Sales Tax licenses
- Seller's permit

Licenses and permits are normally required for three distinct purposes:

- To identify your business and monitor you and the actions of your business
- To protect the public's health, safety, and community plan
- To keep track of you and your business for financial purposes

A successful man is one who can lay a firm foundation with the bricks others have thrown at him.
David Brinkley

Your Business Attorney

Unfortunately, many people only hire attorneys once they have a problem. They try to save a few dollars here and a few dollars there but don't realize that the legalities of their life and business are potentially some of the most dangerous and precarious decisions that they will make!

I always suggest that if you are opening a business you find a fabulous attorney that truly understands you and small business who will be able to protect you and your interests. All too often people try to open a business without an attorney and open themselves up to unanticipated expenses or liabilities that could have been avoided had they spent a few dollars up front protecting themselves!

As a new business, here are some of the things that your attorney may do for you and your business:

- Set up your legal entity
- Review Franchise Agreements
- Review a potential lease
- Draft or review employment agreements
- Draft or review employment handbooks
- Draft or review Trademarks
- Draft or review vendor contracts
- Draft or review partnership agreements
- Send Cease and Desist letters on your behalf
- Argue for you in court

Practical Application

I can tell you a number of stories where our business attorney came in handy. First, we did NOT hire an attorney before we signed our first commercial lease. We thought, "We have a commercial real estate agent; they'll look out for us and make sure that everything is usual and customary." We couldn't have been more wrong.

Mike and I are each licensed residential real estate agents, but we had NO experience in commercial realty so we decided to hire a professional. Unfortunately, we have since found that Commercial Real Estate Agents may not be held to the same standards as a residential agent, and they certainly operate differently in terms of helping you through the entire transaction.

Our commercial agent was a friend, and he didn't really treat our lease with the care that he should have. First, there were a number of places in the lease that were ambiguous or even down right conflicting. The lease should have been cleaned up before we signed it. Second, the lease was written to protect the landlord, and provided us very little options and protections.

To make a long story short, over the course of our lease:

- We were stuck with a large maintenance bill from our landlord for some improvements to their property that should not have been our responsibility.
- A 25-year-old air conditioning unit went out and we were solely responsible for the $10,000 fix.
- There was a significant dispute as to the guidelines for the end of our lease which they felt meant that if we wanted to sell our business, we were legally obligated to co-sign the lease with the new buyer. Because the lease contradicted itself and was ambiguous, the only way to have a clearer picture on the lease would have been to take it to court (a costly, time consuming, and stressful way to get clarity).

Over the course of our lease, it has likely cost us over $25,000 in extra expenses that potentially could have been avoided by hiring a great attorney with a critical eye BEFORE we really needed them! Unfortunately, once a contract is signed, if there are any ambiguities, the only way to clear them up is either through negotiation or the courts. Therefore, it is strongly recommended that you work with a knowledgeable business attorney **before** you begin your business to ensure that you are protecting your assets and are considering potential dangers and pitfalls.

What will be the legal structure of your business?

Depending on your personal financial situation, you will likely want to have some type of recognized legal structure for your business. This is a VERY important part of your business, and is one of the critical places that I encourage you to hire an attorney.

Before you make a decision about what type of entity you want to create, here are a couple of questions to ask your accountant or attorney:

- Does your state have a minimum tax, regardless of net income from the entity?
- Does your state have a gross income fee for an entity, regardless of expenses and profitability?
- Will the entity have "double taxation" (i.e. be taxed on income that stays in the business as well as income that is distributed)?
- What are the tax consequences of selling the business at some point in the future?
- Based on the type of entity, will it be more complicated to sell one type of entity in the future?
- Do I want to be able to distribute to some owners, but not all?
- Do I want all owners to have equal decision-making powers?

- Based on my personal financial situation, what type of entity is best for my family?

I currently have an LLC, but am strongly considering transitioning to a Sub-Chapter S Corp for tax purposes based on our state and my and my husband's income. First, any type of entity such as an LLC, C Corp, or S Corp will provide you a layer of protection from creditors and liability. (A general partnership will NOT protect your assets from creditors and liabilities, so be very careful with partnerships.)

Any time you create an additional entity, however, you may also incur extra fees and taxes based on your state rules. You need to know where you are, and ideally where you want to go.... What is your end game? You can't connect the dots looking forward; you can only connect them looking backwards.

So you have to trust that the dots will somehow connect in your future. You have to trust in something – your gut, destiny, life, karma, whatever. This approach has never let me down, and it has made all the difference in my life.
Steve Jobs

Practical Example

In California, we pay an annual minimum tax for an LLC of at least $800 – no matter what the business actually made in profits. So, if I run a fitness business that has a bad year that makes $600,000 that year in gross income but yet had $650,000 in expenses, we would still pay a minimum state income tax of $800. In addition to a minimum tax, some states also have also a gross income fee. So a couple of years into the business, I was very surprised and disappointed to find that I had a huge fee due because my business had crossed the $500,000 in gross income threshold.

It didn't matter if we had made $700,000 and had $699,000 in expenses - we still owed the state our $800 minimum tax and a $2,500 gross income fee! We will cover the different types of entities to help you make an educated decision. However, I do suggest that you consult a tax advisor and a legal advisor to determine which may be best for you!

Business Structure - Sole Proprietorship

If you don't have employees and the business is just you, this may be an ideal choice. If you use your name for the business and you don't need a business license (to find out if you do, ask your county clerk's office), then there are normally no formal documents you need to fill out for this structure. The profits from your company "flow through" the business and go on your personal tax return, and all of your business expense that are deductible are written up on a form called Schedule C.

If you choose to go with this option, there are a few things to keep in mind. Since you will be filing a Schedule C at the end of the year, you need to keep track of every receipt and go through your expenses carefully with your accountant or bookkeeper. You may be able to deduct your auto mileage, a home office, certain travel, and various types of dining or entertainment. The amount and variety of items that are considered deductible may surprise you.

For instance, a chef can write off restaurants that she eats in for research purposes. A fitness instructor can deduct the classes that they attend. Keep in mind that since you are paid and taxes are not withheld, you will still have to pay taxes on the net income from the business. Depending on how much you make, you may be required to pay estimated taxes quarterly.

Since neither you nor your tax advisor knows how much you will make your first year, these quarterly tax estimates may be more or less than you really need to set aside. If you do not allocate enough toward estimates, however, you may be charged with additional interest and penalties. It is suggested that you consider allocating about 30% of each check you receive toward taxes.

Business Structure – C Corporation

In the past, a C Corp was the most popular choice for many new business owners, but it has recently been replaced by the LLC as the corporate structure of choice. As with any corporation, the C corporation limits liability. This means that if the corporation is sued or files bankruptcy, the corporation is responsible, not the members. This is a HUGE concern if you are running a business with a large amount of risk (for example, a fitness business where you are responsible for the safety of your clients or a business where you rent space and have taken on a large amount of debt/risk); it may be VERY beneficial for you to have some type of legal entity that protects your legal interests.

A properly structured C Corp protects individual assets. A C Corp is relatively easy and inexpensive to form. However, a C corp may be subject to double taxation – with the company paying taxes on the profits, and then the owners/shareholders paying taxes on the distributions from those profits!

Business Structure – S Corporation

With an S corporation you maintain protection from personal liability and you avoid the double-taxation issue that often arise with a C corp. With an S Corporation, all profits pass directly through the entity to the tax returns of the owners without income taxes on the entity. An S Corp is often a business structure of choice for very large corporations and companies that carry large amounts of inventory.

The S Corp operates like any other corporation, with the establishment of officers, directors, and shareholders. An S Corp requires a fairly large amount of paperwork. Like a C Corp, it is more expensive to form than the unincorporated options because you need to hire a lawyer or accountant to file the paperwork for you. Some restrictions apply, and you should review the details with a legal advisor.

Business Structure - LLC

The LLC is a popular option with small business owners because it has the many advantages of an S Corp, including an increase in the number of shareholders you are allowed and the ability to not distribute profits based solely on the pro-rata percentage of ownership. This is now the most popular legal entity type, as it has a lot of the benefits of both a C Corp and an S Corp.

In addition, it is also one of the easier entities to form. Creating an LLC entails drafting an operating agreement and setting out relevant particulars of the operation. There are some disadvantages to this formation; most jurisdictions do not allow LLCs to have only one member. It can be costly, and there are several operating rules that vary by state, so you need to work with an accountant and/or lawyer. For more information, visit www.irs.gov. **Before you decide on the right entity type for you, please consult a legal and/or tax advisor. The money you spend will likely be WELL worth it in the long run! **

Hiring an attorney

Your attorney will be a KEY player in forming your business. If you do not have a trusted legal advisor, consider interviewing 2-3 before you hire one. You may wish to contact your local SBA or SCORE office that can make reputable referrals. They may even have legal advisors on staff that can help you (maybe even for free).

In interviewing attorneys, you may want to ask the following questions:

- What kind of clients do you represent?
- Do you currently work with any small businesses?
- How long have you been practicing?
- What is your area of expertise?
- What do you know about my type of business?
- Do you work with any other businesses like mine?
- What do you see as my biggest legal danger that you can help me with?
- What is your fee structure?
- Are you available for consultation if I pay you an hourly rate?
- Do you bill by the hour, half hour, or minute?
- Do you have references?
- Will I be working with you directly or with a member of your staff?

These questions are all important. First, you want to make sure that they are used to working with small businesses. The attorney for Starbucks has significantly different things to look for than you would in a small business start-up.

Also, you probably don't want to hire a divorce attorney for your lease negotiation. Despite being a licensed lawyer, these two disciplines have very different skills and educational requirements! You ideally want to hire an attorney that specializes in small businesses and their needs.

You also want to know that you will be able to call them for advice. You never know when you may need legal counsel. It is important to have someone that has agreed that they are your business lawyer and will answer your legal questions without having to do 50 hours of (billable) background work to answer a simple legal question.

You want to know if you will be working with that lawyer or if after the initial project you may be passed off to a junior associate with less experience (especially if you are still paying the same rate). For example, a partner in a firm may be who you initially hire. Their rate may be $500 per hour, but you may find down the line that a new associate is the one actually doing all the work and that their going rate should only be $200. They may also need more time to do the research or gather facts than a veteran attorney. In this example, you may be significantly overpaying for the service!

Then finally, you want to know how they are measuring your time. Are they billing and tracking by the minute, or are they billing by the half hour? Imagine if they were picking up your file and doing 5 minutes of work but rounding up to the half hour because of how they bill. That's how a legal bill balloons out of control really quickly!

When you get ready to make a decision on an attorney, ask for references. CALL those references!

Ask the references:
- What type of business do they run?
- How long they have worked with their attorney?
- How responsive is their attorney?
- What has been the most helpful thing their attorney has done for them?
- Do they feel like their attorney has made an effort to understand them, their business, their needs, and their objectives?
- What else should you know about the attorney?

Types of business insurance you need

Despite having a business entity, you still need appropriate insurance coverage to protect you and your assets.

Here are some of the types of insurance that you need to hold:
- Business Liability – Liability insurance will cover you in the event that someone is injured.
- Your landlord will often require that you make them an additional insured on your liability policy.
- Business Property Coverage – This insurance will cover you and your property in the event of theft, destruction, etc. It will cover your computers, tenant improvements, often plate glass, etc.
- Health Insurance – Don't skip health insurance.
- Worker's Comp Insurance – This is paid with payroll to cover your employees in the event that they are injured on the job.

- Unemployment Insurance – This insurance covers you in the event that you need to terminate employees. It will provide them a benefit if they are unemployed.

Free/cheap legal resources:

As a fledgling business, I know that you likely don't want to allocate thousands and thousands of dollars to legal fees. If you need legal advice, you may be able to get some free or cheap, legal advice through your local chapter of Score, your local Chamber of Commerce, or the legal clinic at a local law school.

SCORE is a non-profit organization in many communities that is supported by volunteers or the local SBA (Small Business Association) and offers training, advice, mentorship, and services at a free or reduced price. This is always a first resource any time you get stuck in your small business. They have training sessions, mentors that will help you grow your business, and other small business services as well.

Your local Chamber of Commerce is an organization that businesses may join to network and share resources with other local businesses. The service available to you in your local Chamber of Commerce is dependent on the volunteers in the chapter. As with SCORE, this is mostly a volunteer organization that provides you with training, resources, referrals, and more to help you grow your business.

Finally, a legal clinic at a local law school is an organization that is run by a few law school faculty members. The clinic is designed to allow law students the ability to get some experience with the law and provide free/reduced fee services to the community. Different clinics offer different services. If you are interested in knowing more about their services, look up your local law school and call them and ask about the services that their legal clinic may provide. Often, you must be a resident in that county to qualify.

As you can see, there are a LOT of legal considerations before you open your first business. The ultimate end advice is to hire a legal representative to help you navigate the dangerous and expensive legal waters of starting your new business.

If you took our top fifteen decisions out, we'd have a pretty average record. It wasn't hyperactivity, but a hell of a lot of patience. You stuck to your principles and when opportunities came along, you pounced on them with vigor.
Charlie Munger

**** This chapter is meant to educate you on the legal concerns of a new business owner but is not meant to constitute legal advice. Please consult with an attorney to help you cover your legal responsibilities. ****

CHAPTER 7:
Managing Your Money

Frugality includes all the other virtues.
Cicero

We have covered your personal finances. Once you have those in order, you can tackle the management of your business finances. Many financial decisions/responsibilities will depend on you, your financial situation, your goals, your geographic jurisdiction, etc.

No matter what specific financial decisions you make, I would strongly encourage you to find someone to help you with your business finances. It could be a bookkeeper. It could be an accountant. It could be a financial advisor. Unless you are one of these yourself, you really do need a support system for your finances.

Wealth consists not in having great
possessions,
but in having few wants.
Epictetus

Your bookkeeper or accountant can:
- Help you set up your books
- Help you create a business budget
- Help you create financial projections
- Help you break down startup costs, expenses, obligations
- Help you implement a filing system for all receipts, etc.

- Help you make decisions about forecasting, business growth, and expansion

The key role of a bookkeeper is to oversee the day-to-day books and reporting of your company. They often use a software system, such as QuickBooks, to track all your income and expenses. They will be able to provide you a monthly Profit and Loss Report showing how much you brought into the business vs. how much you spent. They also can show you how much was left over (net profit).

An experienced bookkeeper will often be able to notice the trends in your business and give some insight and advice about the direction of your business, based on the financials. If you are not financially savvy, your bookkeeper may be one of your biggest allies who you can meet with monthly to review financial trends and areas of opportunities.

Where a bookkeeper will likely be part of your day-to-day business operations, the key role of an accountant is to prepare your tax returns and ensure that all appropriate tax payments are made in a timely fashion. The accountant will normally be more expensive than the bookkeeper.

Many accountants consider themselves to be photographers. They take a snapshot of your books at any given moment in time and report on those books to the governing tax authorities. Some accountants also consider themselves tax planners. I am a huge advocate of business owners hiring accountants that consider themselves to be tax planners.

Practical Application

This past year, Mike and I made more money than anticipated – much of it in the last two months of the year. We needed to do some proactive tax planning to reduce the taxes due in the upcoming year. With some quick thinking by both us and our tax advisors, we were able to implement some tax strategies that legally would reduce our tax liability for the year by over $20,000.

Consider an accountant that prides themselves in knowing the tax laws and who feels it is their role to help you legally reduce your taxes as much as possible.

Annual income twenty pounds, annual expenditure nineteen six, result happiness. Annual income twenty pounds, annual expenditure twenty pound ought and six, result misery.
Charles Dickens

You may have the same person/company perform the roles of bookkeeper and accountant. It will certainly simplify your life. Just be aware that you may not have an appropriate level of checks and balances in the business. I have a friend whose bookkeeper was skimming money out of the daily cash deposits. If my friend did not have a separate accountant that noticed the discrepancies in the cash flow reports and the actual cash deposits, this could have gone on for a very long time before it was found! If you are not actively watching the daily cash flow of your business, you may find that you are better served having a system of checks and balances, including both a bookkeeper and accountant.

One thing to be aware of - no matter WHO you hire - YOU and you alone are responsible for meeting the tax obligations of the business.

Practical Application

When I first opened my business, I worked with our accountant to determine the best entity structure for us at the time based on income, expenses, etc. Unfortunately, there was a discussion missed about how much the anticipated gross revenue of the business might be, and over just the course of one year, my gross revenues doubled. A year later we did my first set of business taxes.

I was quite surprised to hear about this fee that would be due each and every year thereafter due to the growth of the business. (Now taxes are normally not altogether a bad thing, because when you're paying taxes, you are likely making money.) In this situation, however, this was a GROSS INCOME fee. This means that, although we had a huge amount of growth in revenue, we had a proportional amount of growth in expenses that first year. We didn't make a ton more money net, but we had a new (and unanticipated) $2,500 annual fee.

Although the accountant should have told us about this in the set up or the next year when we met and completed our first set of business taxes, as the business owner, the buck stops with me! I am the one responsible to the IRS and to the state, and ultimately it is MY responsibility to know my obligations.

No matter what decisions are made, remember – you can delegate tasks, but you can't delegate the responsibility or the liabilities!

I never attempt to make money on the stock market. I buy on the assumption that they could close the market the next day and not reopen it for ten years.
Warren Buffett

If finance, taxes, and reporting are not your strengths - HIRE SOMEONE! Trust me – you'll go crazy if you try to do it all yourself – even if you are super financially savvy! Your accountant can be the person who completes your tax returns, or they can be the person who does your books, pays your staff, AND handles your entire financial life.

When you are hiring your accountant or bookkeeper, you need to consider asking the following:

- What services do you offer?
- How often do you recommend we meet?
- How large is the firm you work for?
- Are you going to be the one managing and working on my business?
- What kind of bookkeeping system do you use?
- Do you have a bookkeeper on staff?
- Are you available for quick calls, or would you prefer that I save questions for our meetings?
- What kinds of clients do you work with?
- Do you work with businesses that are the same size as mine?

- Do you work with businesses that are the same type as mine?
- Based on my needs, could you give me an estimate for how many hours of your time I will need every month?
- Have you ever had to defend a client in an audit? If so, how many and how did they go?
- Do you see yourself as conservative, moderate, or aggressive in your tax preparation?
- If you recommend a deduction, do you believe firmly that you can defend it in an audit?
- How do you charge?
- Do you do bookkeeping and payroll as well?
- Are you a CPA or an EA?
- Are you licensed to practice in _____ state?
- Do you use online systems? How are they protected?
- Will I have access to my books at any time I want them in real time?
- Will I be the master administrator on my account?
- May I have some references?

Practical Application

My entire life prior to opening the studio, I was a financial advisor, and I worked with multi-million dollar corporations. Once I was trying to run my business, handle my personal finances, AND oversee all the finances in the business, I was just too overwhelmed to do it all.

The first three years in business, I filed tax extensions because we just couldn't get everything together fast enough, and that was WITH a professional bookkeeper.

I still oversee the paying of the bills, and I like to track my cash flow. I do that because it is in my DNA. I don't do the day-to-day bookkeeping, deposits, etc., however

Formal education will make you a living;
self-education will make you a fortune.
Jim Rohn

When you are ready to hire an attorney, accountant or bookkeeper, make sure that you get everything in writing. Many of these professionals will provide you with an engagement agreement that sets forth all the agreements between you and the professional. Read the engagement agreement and ensure that the agreement documents are what you agreed to.

Actually, in pretty much any business agreement, you need to get an engagement agreement or a scope of work. Here is a situation I experienced with a past bookkeeper that could have been completely catastrophic.

Practical Example

After being in business over four years, I hired a bookkeeper once who was referred by a friend. The bookkeeper was considered by me to be a friend. When I was looking to hire her, things were often more complicated than it seemed they needed to be, they took longer than necessary, and required more of my time, work, and energy than ever before. We agreed to a fee structure (an hourly rate), and she started on my books. After I hired her, every single thing was more complicated than it had ever been before (and remember, I had worked with business bookkeepers for over four years in this business).

Her first bill came and the amount was almost double what she said it would be, and she was less than halfway through the job. I had to run all the payroll reports for her because she couldn't figure out how to do it. Also, she was operating on Windows, and I was on a Mac. I never had access to my own books!

When I asked if we could go to an online system, she set up the QuickBooks account and transferred the information online. Then she found that she was not equipped to work online. It was more complicated and took more time. By the time we parted ways, my bill was over three times what was estimated, and the work never was finished.

Fortunately, despite being slow, she was honest. Because she had set up the QuickBooks transfer online, she was the master administrator – meaning that SHE had more access to my books and my accounts than I did. Had she been someone else, I may never have gotten my books back! I could tell you story after story of bookkeepers holding their clients' hostage or stealing from their clients – but the clients not really being able to do anything about it!

Money is only a tool. It will take you wherever you wish, but it will not replace you as the driver.
Ayn Rand

What accounting method will I use?

There are ultimately two types of accounting: Cash accounting and Accrual accounting - Once you choose your accounting method, you need to stick with it, so you want to choose carefully. Cash accounting is the most common in small business, and it's simple – you account for income when you receive it, and you account for expenses when they are actually paid.

Accrual accounting is counted when the services or product are rendered, whether you are paid at that time or not. The most significant way your business is affected by the accounting method you choose involves the tax year in which income and particular expense items will be counted. For instance, if you incur expenses in the one tax year but don't pay them until the following tax year, you won't be able to claim deductions for them in the year you incur the expenses if you use the cash method.

You would be able to claim them that year, however, if you use the accrual method because under that system, you record transactions when they occur, not when money actually changes hands. As I mentioned above, Mike and I had to do some creative tax planning this year to avoid a huge tax bill. One of the things that we did was to reach out to all of our vendors and see if we could pre-pay a number of our business expenses. Because we use the Cash Accounting Method, we get the deduction at the time that the expense is paid, not the time it is incurred. So, for us, we pre-paid thousands of dollars in expenses to offset some of our unanticipated income.

Record Keeping

Many new business owners are surprised to find out how much they are able to deduct from their taxes. We deduct much of our dining, our travel, and entertainment. Much of our life is networking, and many of our clients have become long-term clients, referrers, and friends, all at the same time. We deduct our home offices, our automobiles, our cell phones. At the same time, we have been audited TWICE in our time in business! Each time, we have left the IRS agent in less than 45 minutes, with no change, but that is due to our record keeping!

First, we have separate credit cards for each business, and we try very hard to ensure that all bills and expenses go onto our credit cards. It is a heck of a lot easier to track everything when it is in one place! If at all possible, I recommend that you have a single business checking account and a single business credit card. This allows you to track all income and expenses through just two accounts. In the event that you are ever audited, it is much easier to pull out only 24 statements (12 monthly statements on each of the two accounts) than have to pull out statements from 10 different accounts! Also, keep the receipts. If you ever need to produce them in an audit, you need to have them available!

Every single year, I get out a number of manila envelopes. I label them as follows:

- Dining
- Entertainment
- Travel
- Supplies
- Postage
- Banking
- Dues/Subscriptions
- Utilities
- Marketing
- Networking

I take every single receipt and put them in those envelopes. I always have the credit card statements that I use for my back up, but if ever needed, I also have the hard copy receipts as verification. If you are someone that prefers to live in a paperless society, you will want to scan all receipts and save them in a way that you can retrieve them. There are systems like NeatReceipts or Certify that scan and organize them all. Just check the app store on your mobile device and find the best one at the time of this reading!

If you are going to deduct your home office, make sure that it is clear that the home office is an office and not just a bedroom with a desk (or your kitchen). Mike and I each have home offices, and the moment you walk in, you know that they are offices. They have desks, book cases, computers, printers, and video cameras – all the things we use in our business.

Wealth is the ability to fully experience life.
Henry David Thoreau

Business Vehicles

If you have a vehicle that you use for both personal and business use, you want to make sure that you are tracking the miles being driven for personal reasons and the miles that are being driven for business reasons. You aren't able to deduct the personal mileage. We track our mileage every Friday, and break down the miles that were business and personal. (We've been audited on this too, and these records were critical in our defense.)

When you first put a vehicle in service for business use, you need to determine if you will be deducting the mileage on an annual basis, or if you will be deducting the actual expense of the vehicle (the payment, insurance, gas, etc). You have to choose which you will use, and once you choose, that is the deduction method you should use during the life of the vehicle.

In this world nothing can be said to be certain
except death and taxes.
Benjamin Franklin

Paying Taxes

Depending on your type of business and your local jurisdiction, you may have a number of different tax obligations. First, unless you are operating as a sole proprietorship, with no employees, you must register your company and get a Federal Employer

Identification Number. This is a tax number (much like your social security number) specifically for your business.

When your taxes are due is dependent on the type of legal entity you and your attorney chose. Some LLCs and corporations will allow you to have a fiscal year that varies from a calendar year. This allows you some flexibility in allocating income and taxes between different calendar years and may give you more tax planning opportunities.

However, I maintain a calendar year as the fiscal calendar for all my business ventures. I do this mainly because I feel like my financial life is complicated enough. Because reporting and taxes are typically done on a calendar year basis, I would prefer to keep my business reporting on the same schedule!

Payroll Taxes

In my opinion, payroll taxes are one of the worst responsibilities of being an employer. You must withhold federal income tax, state income tax, and sometimes city income tax, depending on where you live, along with social security and Medicare (known as the Federal Insurance Contributions Act, FICA).

As an employer, you also are responsible for matching the employee's contribution to their FICA taxes. Depending on your income and the wages paid to your team, you may need to pay these taxes monthly, quarterly, or annually. In addition to paying the taxes, you must also pay federal unemployment taxes and file an employer's quarterly and annual tax return. Then at the end of each year, you must provide standardized forms and reporting in the form of a W2 or a 1099 to each person who worked for you, and to the IRS and state governing body! Pretty crazy, right?

In case you haven't noticed yet, the theme of this chapter is HIRE HELP! Your bookkeeper can handle your payroll. Your accountant can handle your payroll, or you can hire a company that specializes in payroll! If you hire a company that handles payroll for you, they will normally charge you a flat fee plus a fee per employee/contractor.

Some of the big companies that specialize in payroll are:

- Intuit – www.iop.intuit.com
- ADP – www.adp.com
- Paychex – www.paychex.com

The buck stops here.
President Harry Truman

Practical Application:
The Buck Stops Here

In my time in finance, I had a client with a huge business with hundreds of employees. He had a payroll service, a bookkeeper, and a CPA/tax planner. One year there was a significant change in the taxes due in the business. The bookkeeper and CPA had a difference of opinion on how it was to be handled, and it took them a number of weeks to come to a resolution. In the time that they were basically each researching and arguing, they missed a tax deadline. This disagreement/mistake ended up costing the client over $10,000 in additional fees and penalties.

Remember, the buck stops here. YOU are the responsible party. You can delegate the task, but you cannot delegate the responsibility! No matter what you decide for payroll, bookkeeping, and accounting, I suggest and want you to consider two things:

1. Have someone check your work at least annually.
2. No matter who you hire, YOU are the one responsible for meeting your tax liability. All tax obligations need to be met on time. Otherwise there may be additional taxes and penalties.

I want to end this chapter with a reminder.... I made a recommendation in your personal financial chapter that I want to reiterate here in your business finances. Lead with revenue. There is no better feeling in your business than seeing your bank account increase. And there is no worse feeling in your business than wondering how you're going to meet your expenses, especially if you've maxed out credit cards or have no money available!

Your goal is always to spend less than you make and to have money in the bank as a cash reserve. This will help alleviate stress and will help you continue to build a business that grows! So, no matter WHO is creating your P&L statement, it is your responsibility to review it regularly and make adjustments accordingly!

*You must gain control over your money or
the lack of it will forever control you.*
Dave Ramsey

CHAPTER 8:
Location, Location, Location

> *Real estate is the key cost of physical*
> *retailers. That's why there's the old saying;*
> *location, location, location.*
> *Jeff Bezos, Amazon*

If you are opening a physical brick and mortar location, the location choice will likely be one of the most important decisions you will make. The challenge with a location is that you have to do a lot of the other research (what are you going to offer, who are you going to serve, what type of build out do you need, what are the local demographics, etc.) before you decide on a location.

However, the location you choose may also help you identify who you serve and what you offer. It's literally a chicken and an egg question! Because every type of business is different, I'm not going to cover square footage needs, etc. in this chapter. However, I suggest that if you are going to open a brick and mortar business that you investigate zoning, parking, permits, competition, and complementary businesses before you make final location decisions. However, I do want to cover a number of things that you need to know about renting a commercial space.

> *Silicon Valley is a mindset, not a location*
> *Reid Hoffman*

What are the monthly/annual costs for my desired location?

You often think about rent and just look at the actual price per square foot. However, there may be other costs – such as NNN Triple Net – also known as CAAMS – common area maintenance. My first studio had a rent of almost $2 per square foot. But it also included $1 per square foot of Common Area Expense. These are expenses that you don't control, but they are passed on to you any way!

Depending on the landlord and your lease, there also may be additional costs for cleaning services, utilities, water, signage, etc. So, when you are looking at spaces, consider ALL the costs – not JUST the monthly rent!

The more that you read, the more things you will know. The more you learn, the more places you'll go.
Dr. Seuss

What maintenance am I responsible for and what are the anticipated costs of this maintenance?

In my second fitness studio, – we chose a more industrial space, where literally they cover almost everything in our BASE rent. In my first studio, the lease included NNN (CAAMS) – common area maintenance, PLUS our own expenses for additional maintenance.

In retail centers, the landlord is much more likely to charge you for everything. A retail center lease is typically a lease that includes CAAMS, and the lease often retains the right to make improvements to the building and facilities and is included in your common area maintenance expense.

In my opinion, your location and lease negotiation may be the single costliest business decision. You want to ensure you aren't paying too much nor have large unanticipated expenses. When you are looking at commercial real estate, get in writing any expense. Make sure that you know what maintenance you will be responsible for.

NNN means triple net. That means that basically every single expense of the landlord is passed on to its tenant. Triple net includes taxes, maintenance, and property insurance. This is the most restrictive type of lease and means that basically you are responsible for pretty much each and every expense of the business. In the event that your lease includes NNN, you may incur unanticipated expenses for things such as taxes and property insurance.

Practical Application
Unanticipated NNN Expenses – What If...

If the landlord does not properly maintain the property and is sued if someone is injured, and their insurance rates increase, they may pass that expense on to you (even though it really has nothing to do with you).

Or with NNN, a landlord can pass on property tax increases to their tenants. As an example, if a family has owned a business for many years and has a very low tax base, but during their tenancy they sell the property to a new landlord and the property is reassessed, the new landlord can pass on the tax increase to the tenants of the property.

CAAMS covers the Maintenance part of the triple net (NNN) lease. This allows the landlord to choose pretty much any maintenance that they want on the property and can pass on the expenses to you without your approval.

A Gross Lease is most commonly found in Industrial or office-type spaces. They are the most lenient (and the most predictable) type of lease. If there are improvements that need to be made to the building, parking lot, community bathrooms, etc the landlord picks up the cost. You are still responsible for inside the walls of your space, but anything outside the walls of your space is the responsibility of the landlord.

I have had both a CAAMS lease and a Gross Lease. I'll tell you, a Gross Lease will ALWAYS be preferred by me in the future.

The world is not fair and often fools, cowards,
liars, and the selfish hide in high places.
Bryant H. McGill

Practical Application
Unanticipated CAAMS Expenses

My first barre studio was in a small retail center. I had a five-year lease. Our space was 1622 square feet, and we had our own restroom. About a year prior to the end of our lease, the landlord decided that they wanted to remodel all the restrooms in the center.

Despite having our own in-studio restroom, and not using their community restrooms, we were still responsible for the pro rata cost of the improvements they made to their building. This really didn't seem fair to me.

Over the course of our lease, we were charged when they wanted to replace the trees, paint the center, and replace the grass with turf – all kinds of things to improve their building. We didn't get to vote on improvements. The decision was made, and we were handed a large (unexpected) bill.

If you are serious about renting in a retail center, know that CAAMS and NNN leases tend to be standard. So just be aware and willing to accept that. Also, I'd suggest that you keep a healthy cash reserve for unanticipated expenses!

Each of us is carving a stone, erecting a column,
or cutting a piece of stained glass in the construction
of something much bigger than ourselves.
Adrienne Clarkson

Anticipated Build-Out Costs

The average cost of build out varies WIDELY based on your space, your desired business, and the materials used. Because every business is different, I won't get into all the specifics of potential build-out costs, but I will encourage you to plan out your build out. Draw it out and get estimates on material and labor costs before you sign your lease.

I strongly suggest that any construction is done by a contractor that is LICENSED and BONDED in your state. Although a license and bond still does not guarantee solid workmanship, a contractor that is licensed and bonded has proven that they have gone through rigorous training (and often testing) to qualify. Also, many cities will not give building permits to a contractor that is not licensed and bonded. You would hate to sign a lease then sign a construction contract only to find out that the city won't approve the work and that you are in contracts that can't be completed.

As I mentioned in the Legal chapter, if there is ever a misunderstanding or something isn't completed as agreed upon, the only way to get resolution may be through legal channels. This is a costly and time-consuming way to handle disputes and misunderstandings. Even if you are right, the courts may not always agree. In all aspects of your business, be as clear, concise, and thorough as you can to ensure that all parties agree to all terms.

Get multiple bids and check out your contractor with their local licensing board to make sure that they are licensed, insured, and bonded. Remember, if someone is hurt on your property, even if it is due to the landlord's or contractor's negligence, you will likely be included in any law suit. Choose wisely and carefully! The best way to find a contractor is to ask for referrals.

Your new landlord may have a contractor that they require that you use. You should ask this when you are negotiating your lease. If you have a friend or family member who will do the work for free (but comply with building codes), this is a HUGE place to save some money. Any contractor that you are considering hiring, check them out with the BBB as well as the state licensing board.

Ensure that they will stand behind their work. Let them know that your clients' safety is dependent on them doing the work right. Get a written guarantee on the work they will provide, and don't get ahead of paying them. Pay them a portion up front with the remainder due upon completion. You'd be shocked how often someone stops working on a job – leaving you hanging and often on a deadline.

When we are sick, we want an uncommon doctor; when we have a construction job to do, we want an uncommon engineer, and when we are at war, we want an uncommon general. It is only when we get into politics that we are satisfied with the common man.
Herbert Hoover

Getting Building Permits

Depending on the work you need to have done, you may not need permits, but you need to consider this expense (and timing before you choose a space). A recent client had been negotiating with her landlord for over five months. She had specifically asked about permits, and the landlord said there would be none required. After five months, they came to terms on the lease, and she was ready to sign and start construction the next week, only to find that the landlord and city were requiring a Conditional Use Permit and approval for zoning for her business.

Because of the unanticipated changes, her timelines were pushed back over six months – all over something that she asked about in the beginning of her lease negotiation. As a lesson learned, I would suggest that as you are negotiating with the landlord, and they issue their first letter of intent, get permit requirements in writing. This is a part of the business that you can't really control, but at least you can avoid being blindsided by something at the last minute!

Industrial, Retail, Office

When you are looking for a location, you can choose industrial, retail, or office space. Depending on your clientele and your business needs, you may find that industrial space is the most cost effective and convenient way to go. If you are starting a consulting business that will have a high-end clientele, you likely need to investigate luxury, Class A Office Space.

If you are a photographer with a hip, young clientele, you may find a cool industrial warehouse to be your best choice. If you are a high-end apparel boutique, you may find that a high-end retail center is the appropriate location for you! Get a commercial realtor who can help you find a space and negotiate the lease. They are your representatives, and it is their fiduciary responsibility to protect you and your interests in the negotiation.

You can do a lot of research on potential retail rentals in your area, the demographics of the area, etc from www.loopnet.com. We found each of our spaces by driving around the area we were interested in and then called our agent and asked to see the spaces!

Who else is in the center?

I know that I keep coming back to your target client, but I want you to think about your target client again for a moment while we consider whether or not your ideal space is right for your ideal client.

For a business that caters to women with discretionary income, you are looking for a center that has other businesses that offer high-end products and services. For my barre studio, a shopping center that has a Whole Foods, Trader Joe's, Blow Dry Bar, a Juice Bar, or a High End Nail Salon, would be ideal.

Have you figured out why? THESE are places that your ideal client hangs out. If you are building a business around a physical location, it is EXTRA important that you know your target market, who they are, where they shop, what they do, and why!

Imagine your client leaving your business and heading over to Trader Joe's to pick up their groceries and then heading over for their pedicure, or imagine hosting joint events with these businesses. If you are going to pay for a high end retail center, make sure that the center at least has the type of clientele that you want to attract.

Practical Application
The Day God Saved Me from Bankruptcy

This may NEVER happen to you, but as your business guide, I would be COMPLETELY remiss if I didn't tell you the story of how circumstances saved me from myself! When I decided I wanted to open my first studio, I had my heart absolutely set on one particular retail center as my dream location. When I say my heart set, I think I would have found any reason to go to that center, even if the place had burned down!

Although the center had EXACTLY my target market, it was RIDICULOUSLY expensive, and the numbers really didn't make sense, but oh, I really still wanted to be there. By the time we would have had 1600 square feet, with the rent and the NNN's, our monthly rent would have been over $13,000 per month! If you remember my tip above, NNN's are not altogether ideal.

About six months after we would have opened there, the landlord decided to do a major renovation and would have passed on a lot of those expenses to us through NNN's! In addition, with the significant construction, there was little to no traffic driving or walking around the center. So we would have taken on a huge retail space at high retail rates and expense with none of the benefits. I am not exaggerating when I tell you that it literally would have bankrupted the business! The moral of the story is to not get so focused on one particular spot that it blinds you to the drawbacks. Be willing to see the pros and cons of each and every space.

- Will there be walk-by/drive-by traffic?
- As you are looking at any type of space, you may want to determine if there will be walk-by/drive-by traffic?
- If so, what type? Is it your target market?

When we moved into our first location, we were disappointed to find out that although there was walk-by traffic, it was not our target demographic. Because of our proximity to the beach, we had a lot of vacationers. They may have paid a bit more per class, but they were MUCH harder to market to and impossible to retain! Also, because of some of the restaurants around us, we had a slightly older walk-by clientele than our target clientele.

So, although we had a "retail" space, we were paying more than necessary to reach a clientele that was not really our target demographic. However, had we instead put in an upscale boutique that offered great souvenirs, high-end apparel, women's gifts, etc., our space would have been absolutely perfect!

In our second retail location, we hardly have any walk-by traffic at all! We're on a fairly busy road without a lot of walkers, but we have a ton of drive-by traffic. So we built BIG signs! They are on the walls of the building. They are in the driveway. They are visible from the road, and we have considered putting a huge lighted sign on the roof that can be seen from the freeway! We'll cover this a bit more in Signage. Signage is an investment that if done properly continues providing a return on investment year after year after year, without further investment from you!

When you are investigating potential studio spaces, it is imperative that you consider how people may (or may not) see you.

If you're waiting for a sign, this is it....
Unknown

What type of signage can you get?

One of the potential benefits of a great retail center is the possibility of signage on the road or on your space that will be seen by everyone that comes into the shopping center. If you are in the right space and can get a good place on a monument sign, this could be a huge win for your business. If you can't, however, you may be paying too much for space that doesn't allow you the benefits of walk-by and drive-by traffic – despite the high price tag.

On the other hand, although there may not be existing monument signs, an industrial center may have fewer guidelines on what you can do for signage. In our retail center, our signage had to follow certain standards, and we were always fighting for a spot on the monument sign. In our industrial space, there have been no rules or guidelines. So, when you are looking at space, ask what type of signage you will receive. **Is this space the right fit for my business?** Every single time you look at a space, you need to look at the lay-out and the dimensions and consider:

Does the demographic fit my needs?

_____

_____

_____

Does the traffic pattern fit my needs? Will my clients be able to get to me with ease?

_____

_____

_____

Does the parking fit my needs? Will my clients be able to find parking, or could they leave frustrated and without actually visiting me because they couldn't get a parking space?

_____

_____

_____

Does the square footage fit my needs?

_____

_____

_____

Does the layout of the space fit my needs?

_____

_____

_____

Will the city allow my business to be in this space?

_____

_____

_____

What type of build-out expenses will be required to open in this space?

_____

_____

_____

Is there good walk-by traffic?

_____

_____

_____

What type of signage can I use?

_____

_____

_____

Negotiating Your Lease

Rent Abatement

When you negotiate a commercial lease, know that it is not uncommon that a lessee receives a free month of rent for every year of your lease. This is called rent abatement. For example, if you sign a 5-year lease, you could get up to 5 months of free rent.

Some landlords will give tenant improvements in lieu of free rent, or in addition to, free rent. Please know that this is COMPLETELY negotiable and is one of the reasons it is so important that you have your own commercial agent that is representing you and negotiating SOLELY for your own interests. Review the lease! Make sure that your commercial agent is comfortable negotiating and understands your goals and objectives. If they don't, find another one!

Remember, anything that you negotiate in terms of free rent reduces the amount of money you need up front to be able to open. It also will significantly help with cash flow those first few months when you're getting the word out and building your business.

Tenant Improvements

In addition to rent abatement, you may also be able to negotiate a dollar amount toward tenant Improvements. This is more the case when you will be using the landlord's preferred contractor, but it can be negotiated no matter who you hire! As with rent abatement, anything that you negotiate to reduce your upfront expenses helps you get your doors opened!

If your total construction cost is anticipated to be around $30,000, and you are able to negotiate $15,000 in tenant improvements, then you are only out of pocket the other $15,000! When you are negotiating your space, make sure that your commercial agent has asked for both rent abatement and tenant improvements. They may not get everything, but if you don't ask for it, you don't get it.

I have advised you to hire a Commercial Agent other than the one representing the landlord. Remember that the landlord's agent's fiduciary responsibility is to the landlord. Their SOLE goal is to get the most money and best terms, as quickly as possible for their landlord. They are legally obligated to answer your questions honestly, but they are NOT legally obligated to offer information beyond basic disclosures. They are NOT obligated to look at the deal from your side. Their SOLE responsibility is to their client – the landlord!

Your agent needs to be capable of fighting on your behalf. The landlord may require that you use the funds for certain types of tenant improvements, but as long as they are things that you would have done anyway, that should not be a problem!

The money you need up front

So far, we have talked about rent abatement and tenant improvements. Now let's talk about the amount and type of money you will need. When you go to sign your lease, you will normally need to provide the landlord with:

- first month's rent
- last month's rent
- security deposit (normally equal to one month's rent)

First Month's Rent

The first month's rent will normally be applied to the first month that you owe on rent. For example, if you sign a lease in May and get three months of free rent, you will normally get the month of June, July, and August free, and your first month of rent will be applied to September, making your next payment due in October (certainly helping your cash flow). The landlord will also hold on deposit your last month's rent and security deposit.

Last Month's Rent

The last month's rent will be applied to the last month of rent prior to you leaving the space. So if you extend your lease, you can't use that last month's rent until your actual last month.

Security Deposit

You will also make a deposit toward the security of the property. Your lease agreement will specify under what terms the landlord can hold your security deposit. The security deposit is designed to protect the landlord in the event that you default on your lease or leave the space in "bad" condition. I can tell you that a place that many landlords make some serious money is in keeping security deposits. Make sure that you know what condition the space needs to be returned in, and ideally, that you have photos of when you take possession of the space and when you return the space. We'll cover this a bit later. Photos may just save your butt one day in the future if you're dealing with a landlord who is trying to squeak as much money out of you as possible.

Acceleration Clause

When you negotiate your lease the landlord will likely put in some type of acceleration clause. This is the clause that identifies how much your rent increases each year. It is often based on that area's consumer price index or comparable rates.

It is in your best interest to keep this number as low as possible. The standard is between 2 and 3%, but you want to make sure that you agree to a percentage rate as a CAP. You do NOT want them to be able to say that it will just automatically adjust to current market rates. Make sure that this is written in your lease, that you are aware of what it is and that it is in line with the community.

****Please consult with an attorney before you sign ANY lease agreements. This can be one of the BIGGEST mistakes you can make.****

Option to Renew/Extend

Now let's talk about what happens at the end of your initial term. When you first negotiate your lease, you also have to negotiate what happens at the END of the term of your lease. You need to be very well aware of the terms of your lease and what you have to do to notify the landlord of your desire to extend or to finish out the lease.

Most landlords require that you provide them with written notice about whether you will be extending or leaving at least 3-6 months (90 -180 days) prior to the end of your lease. So, you need to consider well before the end of your lease what you are planning to do. Also, you need to know what your lease states about selling your business and the right to extend/renew. Will it pass to a potential buyer? If so, how?

Practical Application
Plan your "out" before you open...

Your initial lease is what will include your options to renew or extend. You often MUST consider your exit strategy BEFORE you ever sign your first lease! With my first fitness studio, our lease was 55 pages and contradicted itself in a number of different places. Our second studio lease is 2 pages long and very clean and simple!

At the end of the term of our lease, we ran into a problem. We had a buyer for our studio, but the landlord would only let us transfer the business to the buyer if we agreed to personally guarantee the lease for another five years. I don't know about you, but I don't want to personally guarantee anyone else's success! There was no way that I could tie my family's financial future to someone else owning and managing the business.

So to make a long story short, despite having multiple buyers, we were unable to sell the business because of the landlord.

Instead we had to only sell the assets of the business, for pennies on the dollar. Although I knew my goal was only to own the studio for 5-7 years, and although I had an exit strategy, there was a clause in our lease that allowed the landlord to have to approve anyone that would take over the lease - and they decided that they wouldn't let anyone take it without us being on the hook too. This single mistake cost at least $50,000 in lost income at the end of the lease!

Again, please know EVERYTHING you can about your potential lease, and work with a VERY TOUGH and experienced attorney. Spend the money to talk through every "what if" that you can think of! I promise you, it will be money and time well spent!

Taking over someone else's lease

I have talked to many potential business owners who have considered taking over someone else's lease or space.

Pros

There are some DEFINITE pros to this. First, it may already be built out in a way that you were imagining. Second, you may be able to get by without having to come up with the first month's rent, security deposit, and last month's rent. By the time someone wants you to take over their lease, they are often just excited about the possibility of getting out from underneath it.

<u>Cons</u>

However, there are some real concerns that you need to consider as well:

- What if the landlord doesn't agree to you extending after the initial term (many lease agreements state that options to extend are non-transferrable). Imagine building a business for two years and then being told that you can't extend the lease.
- What protections will there be for you to be able to negotiate the rate? The landlord MAY be willing to let you stay – with a 20% increase in the rent (knowing that they have you over a barrel).

There are all kinds of things that COULD go wrong here. So make sure you think them through and discuss them with your agent and your attorney!

Taking Possession of the Space

Your lease specifies what condition you are receiving the space and what condition it needs to be returned in. Unfortunately, the lease doesn't detail every single blemish or detail. It is your sole responsibility to protect your interests as much as possible. The easiest way to do this is to take photos and videos of the space when you receive it. Anything that you think might be "off," get a photo or video of it.

Our lease specified that we were to return the space in the condition it was given. Our landlord tried to make us recover sign awnings when we moved out of our first location. They said that it was our responsibility to remove our awnings and replace them with blank awnings. This may have been true if they had GIVEN us blank awnings, but when we received the space, the awnings had the logo of the other tenant prior to us. It cost us $3,000 to replace those awnings. Then they wanted us to replace them again?

Fortunately, we had documentation from the vendor that we had to recover them due to the prior logos, but without that documentation, it would have been our word against theirs. Again, document everything! Imagine there could be a dispute at the end of the term and protect yourself accordingly.

Returning the space

We're going to jump ahead a few years just to talk about the "what if.". Remember those photos and videos I had you take when you took possession of the space? Review them when you plan to return the space. Make sure that you are returning the space in a condition at least as good as it was when you received it.

Some landlords are looking for a way to keep your security deposit. If you happen to be holding one of those 55 page leases, your landlord is likely one of them. When we returned our space, we replaced a few ceiling tiles, touched up and repainted all the baseboards and walls, and steamed the floors.

We took photos and videos, narrating all the things we improved over the course of our lease and included all of these in our final correspondence with the landlord. We knew, however that our landlord was known for being difficult. So, we were very cautious and kept meticulous records. Just know your responsibilities before you take possession. Again, I recommend that you consult an attorney!

Signage:

Now that you have potentially chosen a space, let's talk about what type of signage to use.

Your landlord may have sign requirements.
- Some centers only allow illuminated signs (normally the most expensive).
- Some require logo'd awnings over the door (still very expensive).
- Some require carved wood (a bit less expensive).
- Some allow printed synthetic materials (normally the least expensive).

In my first retail location we had very expensive awnings. In my second, we were able to do four synthetic signs – with three of them being large signs - for about half of what the awnings cost. Once you identify what type of signs you need, you can search for a local sign provider. Get multiple quotes! This is a place that you can spend too much if you aren't educated about your options.

Do The Work:

If you have found your space, please take a few moments to draw out how you would build out the space.

Not everything that can be counted counts,
and not everything that counts can be counted.
Albert Einstein

CHAPTER 9:
Branding and Website

---

*Be yourself because an original is worth
more than a copy.
Unknown*

We covered how **YOU** will show up in the business and community. Now let's identify how the **business** would show up in the community and to prospective clients.

The branding of your business is mainly the visual aspect of your business. Your branding will include:

- Photography
- Designing your logo
- Designing your business cards
- Designing your marketing materials
- Designing your website

What do you want to portray in all your marketing?

	Strength		Luxury
	Warmth		Modern
	Friendliness		Vintage
	Beachy		Fun
	Retro		Sophistication
	Freedom		

Branding – Your Color Palettes

What words describe how you feel when you look at a brand you love?

_____

_____

_____

Please describe the overall look/feel you are wanting, in terms of colors, general aesthetics, mood, etc.

Colors You Love:

_____

_____

_____

Fonts You Love:

_____

_____

_____

From the words described in the checklist above, which single word REALLY resonates with you.

_____

_____

_____

Now go to www.pinterest.com and type in Mood Board and Color Palette with the colors and feel that you described. Take a screen shot of what you love and put them together to review with your branding professional and web designer.

If you do not feel that you have a tremendous and complete view of how you want your branding to look, I strongly suggest that you hire a branding professional BEFORE you start your website, business cards, photo shoot and everything else. Trust me when I tell you that it is very frustrating and expensive to do a photo shoot, design a website, build and print marketing materials, start creating videos and more, only to decide that you do not feel good about your branding.

Creating your Website

Well, if you have figured out your basic branding and color palettes, you need to start investigating who you will use to build your website. I want to caution you on this. It is one of the most FRUSTRATING parts of opening your business. Web developers are known for being flaky and often taking your money and not finishing the project.

First, you need to determine if your developer is also strong in design. Find a website you love and determine if the developer could not only CODE that website, but could also design one that incorporated your color palette and the visual/emotional feel you want your site to contain. If not, you may want to first hire a web DESIGNER who will help you draw out the design, the structure, and will help oversee someone coding the site. Many websites list the web developer at the bottom of the site.

Website Platforms

Wordpress

The most common platform for websites is wordpress.org. This is a free, open-source platform that allows web developers to build websites, themes, applications and more to build and code websites. The majority of websites are built on Wordpress, as Wordpress is considered to be the most flexible platform at this time. www.wordpress.org

Weebly

Weebly is a drag-and-drop builder that allows you to build your own website. Weebly has multiple pricing options (currently from free to about $25 per month) depending on what you need your website to do. Weebly is a perfect option for someone looking to build their own site and keep costs down to start. Just know that each of these platforms is independent, and you can't switch from a Weebly site to a Wordpress site quickly or easily! www.weebly.com

Wix

Wix is another simple, inexpensive drag-and-drop builder that allows you to choose from multiple themes and customize your website. Wix currently costs between $4 and $25 per month and meets most business needs. As with Weebly and Squarespace, each of these platforms are independent and do not allow the ability to move between platforms. So, I strongly encourage you to choose the platform that is most in line with your needs before you build out a large, full website! www.wix.com

Squarespace

Squarespace is young in the web development world, but they are much like Weebly and Wix – ideal for the do it yourselfer who is low on startup funds. Squarespace has a large selection of themes to choose from and are highly customizable. Squarespace costs between $8 and $26 per month currently and offers the ability to do almost anything you can do on a Wordpress site including SEO, blogging, multiple themes/looks based on the page. www.squarespace.com

Do The Work:

Find some websites that you love and interview multiple web designers'/web developers. Did they design it AND develop it?

Creating an Eye Catching, Easy-To-Navigate Website

Your website is often the first thing that a client will see about your business. It is an evolving, ever-changing, electronic brochure that needs to be reviewed and updated consistently. In my opinion, your website is one of the most important marketing pieces that you will create when you are opening your business.

The positive is that a website is a living, breathing piece. It is typically easy to revise, and if you are just revising data, it can be fairly inexpensive. The negative is that you can spend thousands of dollars on your website, and then just a month later, need to make updates to content, photos, staff, products, services, offerings and more!

So, one of the most important staff people on your team will be your web designer. However, before you hire a designer, it is important that you have a great vision of your website and how you want it to look. Today we're going to talk about the key ELEMENTS of your website. One of your upcoming lessons will be the necessary pages and the content of the site. Great design is a critical element of a fabulous website. Once you know what you love about other sites, you will be better prepared to design your own.

Will Your Website Keep Their Attention?

Statistics show today that the average attention span for a person is 8 seconds. That means that you have 8 seconds to get someone's attention and get them interested in what you are saying. Your website needs to hook them quickly and make them excited to know more. Think of your home page as your first date with a prospective partner! Will you make a first impression good enough that they will want a second date?

Some things that will hold someone's attention longer and enhance their time on your site are:

- Story-Telling Photos
- Short snippets of information
- Breaking up the page with font sizes, smaller paragraphs, and more

Do The Work:

Pick three websites you love.

Website #1:

Web Address:

_____

What I Love About It:

_____

What I Would Change About It:

_____

Is It Easy to Navigate?

_____

Does their site have warm, inviting images?

_____

Does the copy keep your interest, or is it overwhelming?

_____

Does It Say Who Designed It? If So, Who?

_____

Website #2:

Web Address:

_____

What I Love About It:

_____

What I Would Change About It:

_____

Is It Easy to Navigate?

_____

Does their site have warm, inviting images?

_____

Does the copy keep your interest, or is it overwhelming?

_____

Does It Say Who Designed It? If So, Who?

_____

Website #3:

Web Address:

_____

What I Love About It:

_____

What I Would Change About It:

_____

Is It Easy to Navigate?

_____

Does their site have warm, inviting images?

_____

Does the copy keep your interest, or is it overwhelming?

_____

Does It Say Who Designed It? If So, Who?

_____

Easy Navigation in Your Website

Have you ever gone to a website and thought, "I really like their business. Their website really speaks to me," but then you go through the site and keep finding yourself getting lost in the maze of navigation, never really getting the information that you need?

Before you start designing your website, you need to consider what you want your site to do.

- Are you selling something?
- Do you want their contact info?
- Do you want them to call you?
- Do you want them to schedule an appointment?
- Do you want them to watch a video?

What are the main goals of your website? Don't go creating a website with 10 drop downs and 30 subpages. You'll lose the client before they ever get started. Make the site clear and concise.

Do the Work

What are the top three goals of your website?

_____

_____

_____

Elements of a Great Home Page

A business's home page is your first impression. It tells a potential client about you before the client ever arrives! In an ideal world, you would use real photos of you, your team, or your environment, not stock photos. Show them your location, your personality, your clients. Capture the energy of your business. What are the goals for your website? Once you know what your objectives are, you can design the home page.

For example, my Fit in 60 home page is designed for three things:
- To invite someone to be a barre instructor
- To invite someone to open a studio
- To invite someone to schedule a class

This is why when you go to my website, you IMMEDIATELY see those three things at the top. If your goal is to have them join your email list, you want your "opt in" near the top of the page so it is visible without having to scroll down the page. If your goal is to have them schedule an appointment, you want your schedule to be at the top and prominent.

Building Your Email List

Whether you know this or not, one of your primary goals of your website is to get people into your mailing list. Many businesses are driving their clients to social media pages. When I opened my first studio, I did a TON on Facebook and spent quite a bit of money advertising for "likes." The problem with this is that as Facebook changes their system, your followers may be unable to see your posts - making that a less beneficial mode of communication.

If you have their email address though, you can send them email offers, invite them to events and much more! In order to entice them to give you their email address, you may want to give them a freebie (a free video, a free cheat sheet, a coupon) to entice them to give you their email opt-in.

Client Testimonials

We all like social proof, whether we realize it or not. We want to know that we aren't alone. We want others to validate that we are making the right decision. On your home page, consider having at least one testimonial. You can also have a testimonial page of your site, but at least have one testimonial on your home page that directs clients to your other testimonials (or that they can see if they never go to another page on your site). You want one really great and powerful quote that shows clients how awesome you are!

Testimonials with photos are even stronger than a regular testimonial. Video testimonials are the strongest of all. If you can get clients to give you video testimonials, they will do great things for your business!

Your About Page

Your About Page is so important! Google Analytics shows that the About Page is the most visited page of most websites. It tells the client ABOUT you, your business, your staff, your offerings, or whatever you want them to know. It is a very common mistake to write an about page that is stuffy and not representative of the personality of the owner or the business.

Write your About Page from YOUR first person perspective. Write it as if you are talking directly to them. Don't speak in a formal, stuffy way. Speak to them as you would if you were meeting them at a cocktail party.

Make their client experience consistent, and show them your company's culture before they ever walk through your door. This way it isn't like you are strangers when they choose to interact with you further!

- Have great photos and warm images on your About Page.
- Introduce your staff with photos and bios.
- Include your mission statement – tell them what you're all about!

Just show the client what you feel like they need to know before they come to you!

Do The Work:

Write your Bio and About Page.

_____

_____

_____

_____

Your Contact Us Page

Your Contact Us Page is often an afterthought, but this could be another great page for your website. First, your Contact Us Page should be carefully optimized for SEO. This page should list your address, your email address, and your phone number. Ideally, there will be links in this page that allows someone to call you directly from your website, get directions directly from your website, or email you directly from your website.

If you have built in that functionality, you will find that you keep more clients and won't have them bouncing off your web page never to be heard from again. Consider all the ways you want them to be able to contact you and include them. Also, you will often name and describe your location. This is an opportunity to enhance your SEO by describing your street, your shopping center name, your city, other local businesses, etc.

You are confined only by the walls you build yourself.
Author Unknown

Using SEO to Be Found by Clients

SEO is a HUGE part of your initial marketing strategy. It is a free/cheap way to find clients and for them to find you.

- First, list all your offerings.
- Second, list all the communities and neighborhoods you serve.

These will help you identify the proper key words in your website. If someone were searching for you, what key words do you think they will use?

Do The Work:

Make a list of at least 20 key words and phrases:

_____

_____

_____

_____

_____

_____

_____

_____

_____

_____

_____

_____

_____

Determine if you can use any of these key words/phrases on your Contact Us page. Then go and review your other pages and identify if you can weave in additional key words to increase/improve your SEO

Don't build links. Build relationships.
Rand Fishkin

Alt Tags and Meta Data

I may be getting a little deep into SEO, but I feel it is important that you at least understand the basics. I feel that SEO is one of the places that many business owners complain that they were "taken" by unscrupulous businesses charging them an arm and a leg to maximize their SEO, but never really knowing what that meant.

There are two places that are somewhat "hidden" that are SEO gold mines. First is your alt tags – every single time you upload a photo, you need to add a "description and an alt tag" in the settings of the photo that includes your key words. Use sentences that describe your key words and location. For example, I would say something like, "Premier Pilates studio and barre studio in San Diego. Find the best barre class in Carmel Valley."

Same thing applies for Meta Data (which you find in the set up of each web page). The meta data is what Google is going to crawl and display in their Google search results. So you want the meta data to be written to include your key words. Make sure that you write your Meta Data description with full sentences and proper grammar. First, your Meta Data is what someone will find in the search results when they Google your pages. Second, Google has been penalizing pages that just stuff their Meta Data with key words. Use your key words, and (if you are location based) use your location in your Meta Data!

Ultimately, your goal is to have a consistent branding and marketing style across every single media that you use. Your marketing is how you are seen out in the world. Make sure that every single thing you do is in alignment with the branding of you and your business.

I don't really like to call myself a brand and I don't like to think of myself as a brand. I'm a singer, a songwriter, a musician and a performer, and an actress, and all the other things that I do. When you add it all together, some might call it a brand, but that's not my focus.
Beyonce Knowles

CHAPTER 10
Marketing for Moolah

*Marketing without data is like driving
with your eyes closed.
Dan Zarella*

If you're considering going through the trouble of starting a business, you are likely doing it because you want to earn money. Very few people open a business solely for the fun of it. So marketing will be an important part of your business.

When you open your business, there are two things that you must have, in my opinion:
- A website
- A Facebook page

Then there are a few things that you should consider if you have a physical location:
- Brochures/Business Cards
- Coupon Cards (Something with a Call To Action)

Your Facebook page is a free place to engage with your prospects and customers.

*Business only has two functions –
marketing and innovation
Milan Kundera*

Special Events for Increased Revenue

One of the things that you can do to increase revenue in any business that is female-oriented is to host special events. If it's a fitness studio, you can host healthy happy hours or informational/nutritional programs. If it's a women's retail store, you can host "Sip-n- Shops," styling events, or fashion shows. If it's a salon/spa, you can host Mom's Night Out or Pamper Me Happy Hours with champagne and discount services.

Another great marketing opportunity for a business where the target market is women is a special event for a particular type of client. For example, you can host Birthday Events, Mom's Night Out, Bachelorette Parties and more.

Even if you don't run a brick-and-mortar location, this is a great marketing strategy for most business owners. If you are a business coach or online marketing expert, invite your clients and prospects for special workshops, special mastermind events, networking events, holiday parties, or happy hours! Just think about the type of business you want to run and build a marketing/special events calendar around your clientele and their interests.

Back-To-School Events

I don't know about your particular clientele – and you likely don't yet either - but I can tell you that the end of August into the beginning of September tends to be a quiet time in many businesses. This is normally because families are taking their last summer holidays and getting ready for back to school, so all hands are on deck to get everything ready.

I was surprised to find that even my clients that don't have kids were still experiencing some end-of-summer craziness in their lives. This is a great time to offer some pricing specials, short-term workshops or other low price, lower-commitment activities to engage those that have the time and to make some money when your normal activities are slow.

The last couple of weeks of summer are also a time that I spend creating the marketing plan for the final part of the year! The longer you're in business, the more you will start to observe your business cycles and trends. As long as you proactively plan for them, you can make it through the cycles.

In the fitness studio, we host back-to-school events that include free spa services or will incorporate a challenge to try to keep people on task. Many local restaurants in San Diego band together for Restaurant Week where they feature special menus and prices to encourage increased patronage during a very slow time in their business. No matter what your business is, you need to consider the same – how do you even out the peaks and valleys?

Other Community-Building Activities

You can do all kinds of other things to build community and bring people into your studio. Anything that encourages them to mix and mingle tends to be a good thing. Here are some sample ideas:

- Health Programs
- Anti-aging Programs
- Breakfast with the staff with coffee/muffins
- Vendor Fairs
- Corporate Events
- Mother-Daughter Events

There are all kinds of options. I challenge you to go back to your target client and identify the types of events that they would enjoy. Make a list of at least 5-10 events that you could host that you think would create a great community in your studio!

The best way to predict the future is to create it.
Peter Drucker

Grand Openings – Do You Need One and How to Do It

If you have a brick-and-mortar location, you need a grand opening! If you don't have a brick and mortar location, you can still likely do some type of online kick off launch to jumpstart your business! When I opened my first studio, I saw my grand opening as a party to celebrate with my friends and my family.

However, I TOTALLY missed a huge opportunity for free promotion, free press, free food, and a huge opportunity to raise our profile in the community! First, I am going to challenge you to put on your Public Relations hat. Public Relations is basically everything that you will do to be positively known by your customers and community.

So, before you start planning your grand opening, you need to think like a PR expert! Who do you know that can help you raise that profile? Your Grand Opening will offer you the opportunity to potentially pair with a charity and promote your event to their mailing list, to meet a number of different community business owners, get free media attention, and delight and wow your new customers. So pull out a notebook or some paper and start asking some questions.

Setting the Hours of Your Event – Morning

So, when you are planning your Grand Opening, you need to determine what type of event you want to host. The most successful grand openings that I have seen hosted both a morning event and an evening event.

The morning could include activities, raffle prizes, champagne, mimosas, muffins, service discounts, swag bags, or pretty much anything you want to create excitement with the clients. You can get donations for champagne, cupcakes, fruit, juices, etc. You may want to give the attendees from the morning an extra raffle ticket for the evening festivities for some of the fun prizes – or a special prize! Everyone likes free gifts!

You can offer an extra raffle ticket to everyone who brings a first-time friend to the event. Think about your clients and identify how to engage them.

Your Grand Opening - an Evening Event

If you want to host an evening event for your Grand Opening, you can do everything you did for a morning event, but more. Imagine a great party with tons of people and a huge buzz all about you and your business.

For an evening party, you can do class demos (little five minute demos of certain exercises); You can have great food, and you can do a fashion show with one of the local apparel lines and get a cut of all the sales. You can also feature apparel or jewelry lines that you carry in studio.

Some other opportunities for success:

- Gather raffle prizes and sell raffle tickets to benefit a charity.
- Gather donations and host a silent auction.
- Get food donations.
- Get alcohol donations.
- Have a local DJ come spin tunes.
- Have a representative of the charity speak.
- Get media to cover the event – TV, magazine, newspaper, online, etc.
- Invite other businesses with your target client to participate and promote their services.

Getting Donations for Your Grand Opening

If you have really nailed your target client, you know the other businesses like yours that will want to promote to your clients.

These are businesses that will happily donate:
- Items for raffle
- Trial size goodies for swag bags
- Services for a silent auction

They'll donate a ton of things, and if you have partnered with a charity, everything that they donate, they actually get credit as a charitable deduction. So, partner with a charity that you love (and ideally one that has a big list) and start promoting your event. Get on the phone and get donations and participation for the event. Ask the community partners to promote the event for you with their clients too!

Picking Your Charity

We have covered a lot of the reasons you should partner with a charity. but let's now cover THE charity and why! First, pick something that touches your heart! For me, I had a friend whose daughter had cancer, so we chose a childhood cancer charity. You want to promote one that means something special to you!

Second, ask them what they need from you to make it a successful partnership. Is one goal media coverage? Are they hoping for a minimum donation? Third, ask them what type of support they can offer you. Do THEY have any media contacts? Will they promote your event on their social media or in their emails? Once you know that a charity is the right fit, you can start planning better how you'll work together to promote each other and the event.

Getting Press for Your Opening and Your Event

Google some sample press releases for your industry. Here are the things you need to know:

- Have a hook – what makes this newsworthy? When I opened my second barre studio, Black Swan was an Oscar movie and was getting a ton of attention. All of our press releases referenced the Black Swan workout, and we received a ton of interest because of it. Determine what your hook will be?
- Who are the celebrities that do what you offer? Capitalize on that in your press release.
- Is there something going on in your community to tie into?

- Is there a particular time of year that your service is more desired? Why? Can you incorporate that into your press releases?

Marketing is a contest for people's attention.
Seth Godin

Have an Angle!

Your charity is also a great angle. The press loves to support charitable events! Make sure you pitch the charity and invite them to any media events, etc.Do your research. Know who you need to talk to or send your press release to. Send it via email and follow it up with at least one phone call. Keep calling until you get someone on the line. Don't just leave voice messages. Don't give up. It may take a lot of effort but will be worth it!

Do The Work:

Write your press release and do research on who you need to send it to. No matter what type of business you want to open, you will likely need to market. People are often so in love with their business idea that they just don't understand why they don't have a line at the door the moment they open.

What you have to consider before you open any business is how to pre-market your business so you have clients who know about you and are ready to come when you open.

Here are some things you need to consider:

- Facebook
- Twitter
- Instagram
- YouTube
- Periscope
- Press Releases
- Groupon
- Living Social
- Ambassadors
- Bloggers
- Ads
- Flyers
- Cards

Groupon and Living Social

I have business owners ask me all the time if Groupon or Living Social is right for their business. First, I must tell you that it completely depends on the type of business you want to launch! There are some businesses I think discount vouchers are better for than others. For a fitness studio where classes are running, whether they are full or not, I believe that discount vouchers are very helpful when you are first opening.

For a retail store, the required discounts may be too big to warrant the promotion. Also, as a new business, things that may not be part of your long-term marketing strategy may be to get the initial word out about your business when you first open.

First, your main goal is to get the word out about you and your business. What you do need to know is that most of these discount sites require that you discount your services about 50%. Then they will take about 50% of the revenue generated by your offering.

For example, if you are going to offer something with a regular price around $110, you will likely have to discount the item to $55. Then by the time the company takes 50%, you will only receive about $27 – quite a huge difference from your initial $110 price tag.

So, in order to make that work for you, you need some ground rules. Here is what you need to include to mitigate your risk:

- Short Expiration Dates
- Discounts on only certain services/packages/products
- First Time Clients
- One Per Person

Think critically. What is your goal? Is it to be introduced to new clients? So if you are going to do it, offer something to showcase your product or services.

Content marketing is a commitment, not a campaign
Jon Buscall

Facebook Ads to Launch a Product, Business or Service

A great way to launch is to run Facebook ads to a lead magnet and gather email addresses prior to opening. Facebook ads are one of the best ways to hyper target a potential client. If you want to market your services to a 28-year-old woman who makes over $75,000 per year and lives within 3 miles of your business, you can do that with Facebook ads.

Then, I suggest you funnel the ad to a page that they have to enter their name and email address, and then they will have a gift certificate emailed to them. This allows you to capture their email address and allows you to continue marketing to them. Also, if you're giving away certificates for the first week of class, you're filling the studio for that first week of classes and introducing people to your services.

Word of mouth is the best medium of all.
William Bernbach

Referral Gifts

If you're starting on a budget, you want grass-roots marketing as much as possible. A great way to do that is to provide gifts and incentives to those that introduce you to their friends. In addition to meeting a new prospect, you are recognizing and rewarding your best clients for trusting you with their friends and family! This strengthens your relationship with your long-time clients!

Using Social Media to Wow Your Clients

Often when you're opening your new business, your biggest goal is getting new clients! Even business owners that have owned their business for a long period of time are often looking for more clients, too.

When I opened my first business, I was spending over $2,000 per month on marketing - and very few of the things that I was doing actually generated the ROI that I needed in order to make them worthwhile. However, after five years in this business, I have found a LOT of simple, inexpensive things that you can do to increase your exposure and get new clients, without spending thousands of dollars a month.

Increase your social media presence. If you are managing your social media, this is a completely FREE way to meet new prospects.

Facebook

As a business owner, you may be hearing that the Facebook reach has dramatically decreased (which is true), but there are other ways to use social media to engage your clients. Although Facebook has changed how you are able to interact with your fans, it is still one of the most direct ways to reach your target market online. Also, there is no other advertising platform that allows you to directly reach exactly the type of person that you identify as your target market like Facebook does!

Facebook should be a key strategy in engaging with your clients.

1. Set up a Facebook business page.

2. Set up your cover image and profile image. In using Facebook for business, you want to make sure that your business Facebook page is in line with your brand. (Ideally your Facebook page will have the same photos, fonts, colors, etc. that you included in your website and will use across all social media channels).

3. Post regularly with content that your target client will find informational and motivational.

4. Always "close the loop" with a call to action or some way for your audience to interact with you. It could be a link to a landing page that collects their email address in exchange for a discount.

Make it simple. Make it memorable.
Make it inviting to look at. Make it fun to
read.
Leo Burnett

Using Instagram to Grow Your Business

Instagram has become a HUGE opportunity to meet your target clients. Instagram is one of the newer and more hip social media platforms on the block. It works a lot like Twitter with a short message (no real limit on characters, but the messages tend to be short) and a series of hashtags. Rather than being word dominated, Instagram operates on photos and images. Much like Twitter, you have the ability to search hashtags to find people **in your geographic area** who like your type of business.

Just an FYI...You have the same abilities with Twitter as well.

Do the Work:

Create a list of hashtags that you believe your clients are using and run a search on Twitter, Instagram, Facebook, and Pinterest. Open a dialogue with those people!

Hashtags that my clients and prospects would be using:

_____

_____

_____

Using Social Media to Get People Talking About Your Business

Social media does not cost you anything other than time, unless you are paying someone to manage it or you are paying to advertise. Consider creating contests for engagement and sharing. On all your social media channels you have the ability to run contests. You can work with a local vendor who has a nice social media presence, and you can each donate prizes to cross promote each other through social media channels.

For example - you can do a share contest. "Post a photo using our product today, and tag us with the following hashtags (provide a few). Share this on your Facebook, Twitter, and Instagram. Enter as many times as you like. Each week we'll pick a winner."

For all social media discussed, remember that engagement is important. In order to achieve true success in your business, you need to make the clients feel like they matter and that you are accessible and listening to them! Some of the worst social media blunders have been by large companies ignoring customer service complaints on social media.

Schedule Some Co-Sponsored Community Events

When you host an event, work with other businesses with a similar clientele to get the word out. For example, our clients love a few of our local spas and certain restaurants. When we host an event we work with those companies to each donate food, services, etc. and share flyers, social media posts, and invitations across the board. Then when you host your event, give out some marketing materials and offer a special package to the event participants.

Ask them to work with you to market to your similar clients and get the word out. You should be able to reach twice the people with half the effort. You may want to consider joining a local Chamber of Commerce or BNI group that holds monthly networking meetings and shares contacts among members.

Email Providers

Email marketing will be one of the most important ways to interact with your clients. You can build a huge following on Facebook, but if Facebook changes the rules, you may never be able to reach them again. They can never take away your email list or your ability to email your clients, however. Your email marketing should be designed to announce specials, announce events, provide recipes and other great value to your clients! You want to pick a great email provider.

I feel like Mailchimp and Mad Mimi are great email providers. Mailchimp is one of my favorites because the emails look so great, and until your list gets to a certain size, their service is completely free! This is a great way to build your revenues before you start spending too much money! Also, Mailchimp integrates with your website to be an "auto responder" when people opt in to your Facebook ads, etc.

Do The Work:

- Identify how you want to use your email marketing.
- Do you want to send promotional emails? If so, when?
- Do you have great content to provide in your emails that would make your customers excited to open them?

Creating a Content Calendar

An easy way to manage your social media when you are first getting started is to have a plan for how you will deliver content, communicate on social media, promote events, etc.

Here is a sample of a weekly "formula" we use for our social media marketing. You are welcome to copy it, or use this opportunity to create your own.

- Motivational Monday – motivational quotes
- Testimonial Tuesday – share a client testimonial
- What To Eat Wednesday – share a recipe or what you love to eat
- Tech Tip Thursday – share a tip through photo or video
- Friday Favorites – Share something out of your offerings or feature a community partner
- Sunday Funday – Share something FUN!

Do The Work:

A business without a marketing plan won't be in business for long. List the ways that you will market your business and get the word out!

- List 20 ways you're going to market your business.
- How will you use Social Media?
- What will you do to launch your business?

Create a Great Customer Service Experience

Customer service is such an important part of your business. Here are some tips to create a great customer service experience:

1. Listen! When a client has a complaint, don't just try to defend a position. Genuinely take a few moments and hear what they have to say before even considering your response. So often clients just want to tell you their thoughts, feelings, and opinions. If they really want you to do something to help them, they will often tell you what it is they want or need. If you just start speaking, you may totally miss what they are expecting or hoping.

2. Empathize. Try to put yourself in their position. I'm reminded on a daily basis that we all have our own perspective. We find that by genuinely trying to put ourselves in a client's shoes, we can often see something very differently than we would from only our own perspective.

3. Know your product and services! I know that sometimes things fall through the cracks, but try to ensure that all staff members know what is going on and that they can answer clients' concerns. If they cannot, do NOT allow them to wing it. Ensure that the staff is trained to say, "I'm not 100% certain, and I don't want to give you the wrong answer. Would you mind if I check and get back to you asap?" This will keep the client from getting five different stories from five different staff people.

4. Do what you say you're going to do. I'm from the Midwest, and my Dad always told me that someone was only as good as their word. It is so important that if you say you are going to do something, that you actually do it! In our studios, we leave electronic "sticky" notes on the desk top. You can also normally assign yourself a task in your CRM Dashboard.

5. Have specialized staff positions. In our Fit in 60 studios, we have one billing department. If a client has a question about their bill, their membership, etc., the billing requests go to the billing department vs. each staff person trying to handle it. It creates a level of consistency. Rather than having five people posting to your social media, have one person whose specialty is the Social Media scheduling.

Dealing with Client Complaints

You can't keep everyone happy all the time. The best thing you can do is try to create a fabulous experience for your ideal client.

Here are some tips for dealing with customer service issues and client complaints:

- Have clear policies and try to be consistent with them. We all know that almost all rules have an exception, but many of our policies were created because of some type of breakdown in the system.
- Determine those places in your business where things need some clarification, establish those policies and be consistent and fair.
- Have grace with clients. As I just explained, you need to have policies, otherwise you can potentially have anarchy.
- However, you also want to treat clients with care, consistency and fairness. Consider treating that client how you would want to be treated in that instance.

Remember that although policies are in place for a reason, your clients are real live humans who need your compassion sometimes! If you are NOT going to grant an exception, NICELY tell your clients why the policy is in place and that it is hard to offer one person an exception that you can't offer to everyone. Take the time, however, to have the conversation with the clients.

Remember, you can't please everyone all the time. With multiple clients, multiple personalities and multiple perspectives, it is impossible that everyone will always be 100% happy. Customer service is an art that starts with being a great listener and helping find the right solution for the client through great communication!

Using Testimonials to Grow Your Business

If you have run a business for very long, you likely know that a few of the first questions you may get from a potential client are these: What makes your business different?

One of the easiest ways to answer these questions is through testimonials. As human beings, we want to belong, and we want to know that we are like other people. Testimonials are the "social proof" that other people like you and that you are worthy of someone else's (a new client's) trust.

There are multiple ways that you can use testimonials. Use your iPhone (or other smart phone) to get video testimonials from your clients. You can literally film the video and upload it to your social media within 10-30 seconds - without it costing you a dime. In addition to using the video testimonial and posting it to your Facebook page, you can edit it to make it shorter, hit the highlights, and make it a short Instagram video. You can post the videos to your website, LinkedIn, YouTube and more - ALL for free!

Ask them to give you written testimonials and photos (Photos make testimonials much more powerful). You can do this through a Client Feature where the client tells you about themselves, their life, and what they love about your business. You can then use these features to post on your Facebook page, as a photo with words on Instagram, and as a photo/with words on Twitter. You can also use these testimonials on printed materials, flyers, etc., providing social proof for you and your business each time that you interact with a potential client.

Getting Client Reviews

Reviews and testimonials have a huge impact on your business. Ask your clients to give you Facebook, Google, and Yelp reviews. As a business owner, Yelp is a double-edged sword. It can give you tremendous visibility and set you apart from the crowd. It allows potential clients to get a peek into your business before ever meeting you.

On the negative side, as a business owner, you may have heard, "If you don't do this, I'm going to give you a negative Yelp review." In my studios, we offer a Groupon or Living Social voucher to first-time clients. All our vouchers specify that they are for first-time clients. One day, last month, I had a client buy multiple vouchers and then say that if we didn't honor all her vouchers she would give us a negative Yelp review. In that case, there is just no reasoning with a client. All you can do is surrender or take the negative review.

By getting tons of great reviews from all your happy clients, that one anomaly will stand out as an anomaly and won't harm your online reputation. You must, however, take charge of your online reputation and interact on all review accounts. Take the reviews that were given on your review accounts and highlight them on your social media! These people have taken the time to note what they love about you and your business.

Create Testimonial Tuesday or something of the sort, and highlight a fabulous testimonial once a week on your social media, in studio, etc. Reference your reviews and your testimonials in as many of your marketing pieces as you can. Again, reviews and client testimonials are a COMPLETELY FREE way to build your reputation and your business! Use them!

Marketing Never Stops

Marketing is imperative when you are first opening your business. But marketing will continue to be part of your business responsibilities until the day you close your business. It could include referral programs, it could include social media, and it could include advertising. Marketing has changed so much in just the past five years, and it will continue to evolve and change in years to come. In order to continue to grow your business, (this seems unfinished).

A lot of times people don't know what they
want until you show it to them.
Steve Jobs

CHAPTER 11:
Staffing for Sanity

Staffing is one of my biggest shortfalls in my business. Because I lack patience, I don't like dealing with staff any more than necessary. However, I know that it is a necessary "evil" of my business (and likely yours). So, before I start giving you a lot of staffing advice, I will start with a series of questions.

It may be hard to answer all of these right now, but as we have already discussed, it is important that you have thought of your big picture goals before you just dive into hiring! Your team will either help you grow your business or they will create extra work in your business!

Do the work:

Where do you want to be in your business after a month?

_____

_____

_____

Where do you want to be in your business after six months?

_____

_____

_____

Where do you want to be in your business after a year?

_____

_____

_____

Where do you want to be in your business after 10 years?

_____

_____

_____

Are you prepared to manage staff? Is that something that you feel you will do well?

_____

_____

_____

Here are some of the staff members/mini teams that you may need to build or grow your business:

- a marketing team
- a social media manager
- a PR team
- a cleaning staff
- a personal/virtual assistant
- a book keeper
- an accountant

First, you need to know that the first time you hire staff, it will be scary. You may know that you need the help, but you don't know that you have the revenue to support the new staff. You may have never been a manager before and don't have any history with managing a staff and getting the most from them.

I have a number of friends who have told me that it was downright painful to hire their first staff member. They knew that they needed it, but they just didn't have the confidence that they had enough revenue to support a staff member. At this moment, I have a full time salaried manager in my fitness studio. But it took me almost five years and a whole lot of staffing FAILS to get to the point that I realized that it was COSTING me more to NOT have the right staff.

Practical Application:
The Importance of the Right Team

Over the past year, leading up to hiring a full time manager, I hired a part time marketing person and had four different part time people in the studio. During those six months, that team brought on only three new members over a total of six months. There were too many cooks in the kitchen, and not enough consistency to really see relationships and sales through start to finish. So, our clients weren't connecting to the staff, and sales just weren't happening.

After hiring a full time manager, and re-evaluating the sales system, she has been able to step into the studio and completely change the sales system to work for her. In the time that we revised the system to better fit her and her sales style – she had eight new memberships in her first month and five in her second month. Her wages are about twice as much as the part time staff (a difference of about $1500 - $2,000 per month), but with eight new members at JUST a $600 value over six months, she brought in over $4,800 over just that first month. (And this is assuming that these members are only members for six months). It is scary to take on that first staff person, but this is just one example of how it can help you!

Second, if you are not quite ready to take on a full staff person, you can always look at part time help or maybe even a virtual assistant. A virtual assistant is a GREAT and lower cost way to put your toe into the water with a potential staff person! It also allows you to hire a few potential part time team members that are highly specialized in different tasks and skills.

Here are a few ways to know you are ready for a staff member:

- You know deep down that you need help.
- You know you can't do much more.
- You know that someone else can likely do the tasks better than you can.
- You have hit a place in your business that you know that you can't grow as long as you are the only one doing the tasks.

Do The Work – Are you ready for a staff?

Do you feel too busy/overwhelmed by your current work load?

_____

_____

_____

Are there things that you do in the day that you feel you could offload to free up time?

_____

_____

_____

Are there high impact/revenue increasing activities that you could be spending your time on by outsourcing other tasks? (High impact activities are those that will improve your product, service, or income).

_____

_____

_____

Activities that you could be doing that will improve your product:

_____

_____

_____

Activities that you could be doing that will improve your service:

_____

_____

_____

Activities that you could be doing that will improve your income:

_____

_____

_____

What daily tasks do you feel will have the biggest impact on your business? (Spend your time here.)

_____

_____

_____

What tasks do you LOVE to do that you would like to spend more time in?

_____

_____

_____

What tasks do you HATE to do (that you would love to pass to someone else)?

_____

_____

_____

What tasks do you know that someone else could do better and faster, and if you paid someone else to do it that it would make you more money than it would cost you?

_____

_____

_____

Any time you are looking at your staff, what you open a business with may not be the same staff you have in a year. Your hours of operation at the beginning of your business may be less. But you may need more marketing support. You may need to hire someone to help you set up your website, your social media, or PR.

Then once you know what you need today, you want to at least be mindful of your goals and objectives a year from now to determine which direction you're going. Also, if you know what you're looking for, you may find the best staff people just out and about in your day.

One of my best in studio hires was working in a high end retail store in one of our San Diego malls. She was warm, friendly and very proficient of showcasing certain merchandise and trying to get you to buy more! Her customer service was amazing! As we were in the store, Mike said to me, "You need to go talk to her and give her your business card. She would be great in the studio." I said to him, "I can't go poach someone else's employee right out of their job!" So, I didn't do anything. Surprisingly about a month later, this high end store sent her as a representative to an event in our studio. I was able to talk to her one on one that day and she was working with us two weeks later. It was a very serendipitous series of events. But I almost let a great opportunity pass me by.

If you don't have a plan for your staff, you won't know a great opportunity or a great potential staff person even when they are sitting right in front of you! Depending on your business, you will have a variety of needs. One thing I want to make sure I tell you now, **I am a huge advocate of having TOO MUCH staff.**

I'm not saying be wasteful. But I believe that you always have things that can be done to improve your business. You never know when you will have someone drop a bomb on you that they will be moving in two weeks, or they took another job and today's their last day.

As I have transitioned from spending the majority of my time in the studio, I have hired more and more personal, administrative, and virtual assistants.

Practical Application
Have Plenty of Staff

Just recently, we hosted a Christmas party for our staff. The next day, my part time personal/administrative assistant was supposed to arrive at 10 am to work with me. I had a list a mile long of things that I wanted her to be working on, especially as we're closing out the year. But at about 10:45 I hadn't heard from her. I texted her and asked if she was coming in. About an hour and a half later, she called me and left me a message that she had been offered a full time job that morning and they wanted her to start that day. She said that her family needed the money and she really needed the full time work. She asked if she could still work with them full time and work with me on the side.

First, after she didn't show up at her shift that morning and didn't have the good sense to tell them that she needed to give me some notice, "Ummmmmm.... No." But second, this person was working for me only part time because I had observed that after about four hours, she stopped working and would either be ready to go home or she would start surfing the internet. She didn't have the attention span to work with me full time in what I needed!

Fortunately for me, I have two virtual assistants in the Philippines (that I'm paying a third of the wage to) that were able to take over many of the tasks within 24 hours. If I did not have depth in my staff, I would have been completely stuck!

Ultimately it ended up saving me some money, but it certainly caused me some frustrations and headaches, as some of the tasks had to be done on site and just couldn't be done remotely, and rather than paying someone $15 an hour, I was left doing the tasks, when my time would have been much better spent doing other things!

The point of this story is that you never can anticipate when your staff will change and someone you were counting on won't be available any more. So, you need contingency plans and growth plans if possible. And in an ideal world, your staff will be cross trained in such a way that they can cover for each other as needed!

And if you don't have enough staff, you might end up having to cancel a vacation that has already been paid for to an All Inclusive resort in Mexico to cover your business. TRUE STORY – This happened about six months after I opened my first studio. Nothing like losing THOUSANDS of dollars and the trip you had been counting on to save your sanity! ;-) So, make those contingency plans....

Do The Work:

Who will do what tasks in the business? If one person (the main person isn't there to do the tasks, will there be someone else behind them that can pick up the slack?

Who will do these tasks:

Facilities	
Cleaning The Location	
Ordering Supplies	
Maintaining Facility (light bulbs, repairs, etc)	
Computer Maintenance	
Locking Up	
Digital/Social Media	
Creating Website	
Updating Website	
Managing Facebook	
Managing Twitter	
Managing Instagram	
Managing Pinterest	
Creating Brochures	
Marketing	
Canvassing Area	
Cross Promotion	
Scheduling Media	
Getting Press	
Creating Enewsletter	
Client Follow Up	
Creating Presentations	
Scheduling Presentations	

Customer Service	
Managing The Schedule	
Serving The Customers	
Booking Travel	
Finance	
Payrolll	
Paying Bills	
BookKeeping	
Tax Payments	

How much should you pay your staff?

Ok, so I am to one of the dreaded questions, and answers. And I always tell people that this question can vary across the country and varies widely on the skill set you require.

Admin:

An admin position could vary at between $10 - $20 an hour. Because the position is normally based on the completion of tasks, the compensation will normally be based on the hours worked and the tasks complete.

Sales:

A sales person needs to be compensated (well) on what they sell! You don't want your sales staff to be compensated too heavily based on time. You want them to be compensated on meeting sales objectives. And you need to set sales incentives and quotas. Not too long ago, I had let the quotas of the studio slide. As such, the staff stopped selling. As soon as I called them on the lack of sales and told them that positions were going to be eliminated if the sales quotas were not being met, the sales team really stepped up.

One of the biggest mistakes that you can make with a sales person is to pay them too much in their base income. You want them to be eager and hungry to sell and you want their sales compensation to be a key motivator FOR sales!

Web Design

My web designer is about $100 an hour. This is a bit more than I have paid in the past, but she is well worth it. If you talk to business owners about their experience with web designers, you will likely hear horror stories of how the business owners were overcharged or maybe never even received their final product.

Practical Application
Web Designers and The Big Danger You Want to Avoid

A few years ago, I hired a web designer who came referred to me from my business coaching group. The designer was a bit pricey, but she really seemed to know her stuff. She created the design of my new site, and I loved it! She totally understood what I was trying to accomplish and captured it in the design of the website.

Unfortunately, she was taking a really long time to get the task done. The agreement said it should take a total of four weeks to complete the website start to finish. After eight weeks, I kept getting excuses of why the project wasn't done. Then, despite the project not being done in a timely fashion, she tried to change the terms and wanted to increase the price substantially. When I said no, she hijacked my website and my social media accounts. She changed the passwords and made it where I couldn't get into my own things.

Fortunately, I still had a master administrator account on my website that was not visible from her place in the site. Otherwise, I may never have been able to get my website back without legal action.

There are a few morals to this story…

1. Always keep control over your own data. There is little worse than not being able to access your own data.
2. Make sure that your contracts are very clear about expectations (scope of work and the cost).
3. Only work with people you trust. If you have a gnawing feeling in your gut, listen to it!!!
4. It is often worth it to pay a bit more for someone great!

Practical Application
Staffing – Listen to Your Gut

Not too long ago, I hired a girl in the studio to work with us in marketing and sales. I did it against my better judgment. I knew better! She was absolutely the most qualified person for the position. But there was just something I couldn't put my finger on that told me that she wasn't the right fit.

I interviewed her four times over the course of the month. She was so qualified that I desperately wanted her to be the right person for the job, despite knowing in my bones that there was just something that was "off." I kept pushing that feeling aside and hired her anyway. And immediately, on a daily basis, I was finding big reasons to fire her!

You see, she wasn't a culture fit. She was great about calling corporations, but she didn't speak to the staff or the clients in a way that was congruent with our business. She also took very little responsibility for anything beyond tasks.

Every single night, I went to bed thinking about how she wasn't the right fit. The final straw was only a week after she started. She came into the studio while I was there teaching because she wanted to use the computer. She sat on the bench fiddling with her phone. She didn't engage anyone in conversation and when it was apparent that the computer wasn't available at that moment, she left in a bit of a huff and said she was going to run some errands and would be back later. She then left hours prior to when she said she was going to be leaving. But despite not being there doing the work, she was billing for the time that she ran personal errands and the time after she left. And when I asked her about it, she said that she had been there at times when others could verify that she had not.

There was an integrity problem. Fortunately, she knew as well as I did that this was not the right fit. But I wasted time and money training a staff member that I knew all along that I shouldn't be hiring. It was just plain stupid – and I knew it all along the way. The moral of the story… Follow your gut. If you know deep down that something is not right for you or your business, don't do it!

Other Technical Skills

I have a very complex CRM system that requires a specific set of skills. I can hire a virtual assistant in the Philippines to do a large number of the tasks for $5 - $10 per hour.

But when I hire a United States based professional, the going rate is about $125 – $250 per hour for someone who is very proficient in the software! As you can imagine, the monthly costs can REALLY add up! If I have 30 hours of work at $10 per hour, it will cost me $300. If I have 30 hours of work at $200 an hour, that will cost me about $6,000!!!!

Also, I believe in incentivizing behavior. I will cover this a bit more later, but I believe that you would prefer to have a competitive base and pay staff more to in incentives for things that you really want to focus on and you want done in a certain way! For example – our admin/reception team can make between about $12 - $15 per hour, but then has the following incentives.

The reception team receives incentives for:
- Working together as a team to make sure that all the shifts are covered and not dropped in my lap.
- Membership sales
- A monthly sales goal that pays them more when the studio hits a certain gross revenue.

I have incentivized the behaviors that I want to encourage. And the better they all do, the better they make! They are compensated on their individual sales. But they are also compensated as a team because I believe that the team must work together for the studio to be successful.

Payroll and Bookkeeping

If you didn't read the chapter on managing your business finances, I'm going to give away the end of the story.... HIRE THIS OUT!! But ultimately, the question is do you want to try to do everything yourself?

- You can manually cut checks, make deposits, and fill out quarterly forms.
- You can hire a book keeper to run payroll.
- You can hire a service to run payroll.
- You can hire someone to pay the bills.
- You can hire someone to manage all your finances.

Unless you are a trained accountant, I strongly recommend that you either hire a payroll service or have a book keeper that helps you (or you hire both). But if you have staff, the paperwork involved in managing all the legal and financial responsibilities manually is CRAZY!!! Take my word for it – don't do it.

As an employer, you are legally responsible for:
- New hire paperwork
- An I-9
- A W4
- A W-2
- A 1099
- Worker's Comp Insurance
- Unemployment Insurance
- Fica
- PLUS all the federal and state quarterly and annual forms.

Unless your previous life was accounting and you miss it – hire it out.   ;-)

Will your staff be employees or independent contractors?

In most cases, your staff will be a series of people that you control what they do, when they do it, and how they do it. If this is the case, they must be employees. Over the past few years there have been a wide variety of companies sued by staff or fined by the state for misclassifying employees as independent contractors.

A few things that almost always make a staff person an employee:
- You want to create and control their schedule
- You control their job duties.
- They are required to be there at a certain time and leave at a certain time.
- They may be handling administrative tasks for you.

Therefore, they need to be paid ether hourly or could potentially be salaried based on the time that they will be working. Because each state has different requirements I suggest that you work with a legal advisor or payroll team in setting this up.

How do I measure my staff's performance?

I've mentioned before that your staff is one of the most important aspects of your business. A good staff can MAKE your business. A bad staff (even one bad egg) can BREAK your business! I know of a fitness studio owner who oversaw their staff by installing video cameras and watching what they did in the studio. Then they would text the staff to complain about all of the things they did wrong. Not the best management style, right?

Would you be surprised to hear that her staff didn't enjoy working for her and that people rarely stayed more than a few months at a time.

Leadership and Company Culture

One of your biggest roles as the business owner is to be the leader of your team. You can be a very visible leader who is physically on site a large part of the time. You can you're your team through staff meetings. You can lead your team through emails. You can lead your team through video. But you are the leader and your team is looking to you for leadership.

Here are four ways that you can be a great leader:

- Be kind, warm, and friendly.
- Help your team solve problems
- Take the time to get to know people and provide real solutions, not just a canned solution
- Help your team and clients feel GOOD when they interact with you.

Your team is YOUR PERSONAL biggest "client". They are your representatives when you aren't there. And they are often part of the face of your business. It is important that you treat them as such. According to Robert Hogan, researcher and author of Personality and the Fate of Organizations, it is believed that 75% of the workforce feels that their boss is the most stressful part of their job.

One of my favorite leadership books is *People Follow You* by Jeb Blount. He does a great job describing what constitutes true leadership. You can have no "power" at all and be a fabulous leader. Or you can have all the power in the world and be a lousy leader.

I believe that if you have to state your position then you have already proven that you are a lousy leader. For example, I once had a manager who could never get any respect from a couple of staff. She believed that everything had to be done her way and she was often a bit obnoxious in her delivery. As one of our instructors was carrying on a conversation with the class, the manager came in and said to the instructor, "It's time to start." When the instructors said that they were waiting on a couple of people in the restroom, the manager said, "But I'm the manager and I say it is time to start." If you have to declare yourself as the manager, chances are you aren't a very effective manager. You are normally declaring your position or your title in the effort to get someone to "obey" you. AIt doesn't work that way! If you have to say that "I'm the boss of you", then you're likely not really the boss of them!!! One of the main principles of *People Follow You* is a comparison of Leading, Managing, and Coaching.

In a nutshell:

Leading is shaping your company through your vision. Leading is inspiring them to get on board with your vision and mission.

Managing is shaping your company through systems and direction. Managing is about giving specific instructions and expecting them to be followed.

Coaching is helping to train, encourage, and empower your company through time and feedback.

There is a time for all, but in an ideal world, the more you can lead, hopefully the less you will have to manage! If you want people to follow Jeb Blount so keenly states that "If you want people to follow you, treat them in a way that will cause them to WANT to follow you!

Keeping Staff Morale High

Staff morale is important to the success of your business. When your staff is no longer engaged or excited for the success of your business, you will start to see sales drop off. I can tell you this from experience! Your leadership will often mean the difference between significant success and mediocre success!

To be an effective leader, create a way to communicate with your team! You can use technology such as a private Facebook group to create communication channels for your team. In an ideal world, you would have a monthly or quarterly staff meeting and give some group training and feedback. You may also choose to have a monthly/quarterly team building social event. This is a great way to get to know your team as people, have them see that YOU are a real person (not just their boss), and it helps them get to know each other better to work as a team!

If you have the time and can manage it, I suggest taking each staff person out at least twice a year individually for coffee, lunch, dinner, or a cocktail to get that personal touch with each staff member!

If you are not actively involved in the management of your business, that is totally ok. You can absolutely hire a manager oversee the team and host these meetings. But make a point of offering the staff the ability to get to know their supervisors (and vice versa) as real people with real families, goals, dreams, and challenges of their own. You will find that your team will be much more cohesive when they know and understand you, your mission, your vision, and their teammates!

As a general rule, I HATE reality TV. I hate the fact that The Real World basically killed MTV as we knew it. I hate that we are all so entertained by watching train wrecks and people making complete idiots of themselves. But I do occasionally enjoy sitting down to watch Undercover Boss. I am guessing that much of it is staged, but I do love the entire concept of a CEO of a large company leaving their office (where they are often out of touch with what is really happening at various levels in their business) to go and meet various staff members. There are a number of things that can happen! First, these CEO's get to meet their staff and get to know them as real people. Second, they often see systems that are ineffective or broken! Third, they get to revisit the vision of the business that maybe they have lost across the way!

When we start a new business, we normally have big dreams of what we anticipate happening! But in the stresses of the day to day, we often forget what we started out doing and why! Your vision and mission for the company need to be BIG! And they need to be communicated often to your team! Your team needs to know that you care about the company, and that you care about them! But also, they need to know what is expected of them.

I've mentioned already that I am a huge believer in incentivizing behavior! You can keep morale high, but really – your staff will work harder for you if you incentivize them to work harder for you. It could be incentives in their pay or it could be other gifts or perks. These incentives literally can mean the difference between you having a life of freedom or you being chained to your business 24/7.

In order to get your team to "work harder" for you – they have to really believe that what they are doing matters. If it is just a job – you're going to get exactly what you pay them for. But if you incentivize certain behaviors – marketing metrics, sales metrics, teamwork – things that are in line with the vision of your business and your goals, then they will WANT to work harder for you. They will want to help you succeed. But the staff needs to know what is important to YOU! They want to know what the expectations are.

In your business plan, I suggested that you write a mission statement. This is a great time to revisit that. Make sure that your staff knows your mission. Share client success stories with your team! It gets them excited! It helps remind them why they are working for you or what they are trying to bring to your clients! If you run a brick and mortar business, I'd suggest incentives based on new clients, sales, gross revenue, net profits, teamwork, etc.

If you run an online business, you may want to consider incentives based on the team meeting deadlines, list building, and sales! And the absolute best way to incentivize an online business staff is to give them a cut of sales! Although I have also seen some online business owners incentivize their staff with new computers and fabulous vacations!

In addition to compensation incentives – consider a staff person of the month – or something that provides recognition to the team for a job well done!!! It can be a Kate Spade purse. It could be a spa gift card. It could be a two-night trip for the winner and their significant other! Just pick something that will get them on board and excited for the mission of your business!

Recently, I had a fellow business associate (we'll call her Haley) tell me that she had an amazing staff person that she really wanted to incentivize. But Haley didn't feel that she was ready to increase her compensation in the long term. So, we sat for about a half hour and talked about this particular staff person and what may be a great fit for THIS staff person! Haley wanted to personalize the incentive in such a way that it showed that it was chosen FOR this staff member. Ultimately, Haley decided that she was going to create an incentive on the next product launch (in addition to the incentive compensation) that would provide this staff person with a new Macbook if they achieved their sales goals. Do you think that this staff member worked hard to achieve those goals during Haley's launch? You bet she did!!!! She took a LOT more ownership in the success of that launch, and put in a LOT more work. That $1,000 would have been appreciated as money. But it was WILDLY VALUED as a new computer!

Homework:

Design a potential incentive plan for your staff:

What behaviors do you want to encourage in your staff?

_____

_____

_____

What behaviors do you want your staff to avoid?

_____

_____

What perks will excite your staff?

_____

_____

What will each of these perks cost?

      Perk #1: _____
      Perk #2: _____
      Perk #3: _____
      Perk #4: _____
      Perk #5: _____

Are there some perks that you can get from free? In my women's fitness business, we have a number of vendors that are always looking to get their products and services in front of our clients and instructors. We have had a number of them make donations to our staff as perks.

Are there any perks to offer that would excite your staff that don't cost you anything?

Free Perk #1: _____
Free Perk #2: _____
Free Perk #3: _____
Free Perk #4: _____
Free Perk #5: _____

Performance Reviews

Your team probably craves feedback. As business owners, we often feel bad providing negative feedback. That's normal! But your team needs to know what they are doing well and what they need to improve upon! The best way to implement regular feedback is to implement a semi-annual performance review with each staff person!

This allows you to provide feedback on the things your staff is doing well, as well as where they have room for improvement. You want your review to touch on the past as well as the future.

Here are some sample questions:

- What worked well?
- What could be improved upon?
- What are your goals for the next six months?
- What do you need from me or the team to help you over the next six months?

If you include a small wage increase or a perk/gift each time you meet with a superior staff person, they will constantly be looking forward to these, and the performance review will be seen as a positive, not a negative! (This doesn't have to be a lot of money or a huge gift – just something to show that you appreciate them.) OR have some type of fun bonus/gift for the staff rock stars during their performance review. ;-)

PERFORMANCE REVIEW

To Be Completed by Staff:

If we were sitting here a year from now and you've had a GREAT year…. What would that year look like?

_____

_____

_____

What have you accomplished?

_____

_____

_____

What are you working toward?

_____

_____

_____

What has the company done to make your job/life better?

_____

_____

_____

What have you done to improve the company?

_____

_____

_____

What can you see that the company can do to improve their product or service?

_____

_____

_____

PERFORMANCE REVIEW

To Be Completed by Employer:

Biggest strengths:

_____

_____

_____

Biggest dangers that we have seen:

_____

_____

_____

Biggest areas of opportunities that we have seen:

_____

_____

_____

New policies/procedures for you and the team:

_____

_____

_____

New goals/projects for you and the team:

_____

_____

_____

Other changes, announcements:

_____

_____

_____

Do you know your state employment laws/obligations?

We talked about hiring a payroll company. The legal obligations of running your business are HUGE! Every single state has different employment laws.

As a basic set of rules, you are responsible for:

- paying the staff at least minimum wage
- determining if you have to offer health insurance
- carrying unemployment
- paying social security benefits
- and more

Some of these payments are due quarterly, some monthly, some annually.

You also need:

- a legal offer letter
- an employment contract
- an employment manual

These documents are literally the "Cover Your Ass" documents of your business. I know a business owner who did not have an employment agreement or employment manual. They were sued for over $400,000 based on not meeting their legal requirements. Had they had a clear employment contract, there would have been little to no confusion about the position. Remember that it is important that all obligations are met and that you meet all disclosure, reporting, and legal requirements! The staff person that seems like the perfect staff person today may be your horror story a year from now.

The Importance of Job Descriptions

One of the things that I found in business ownership is that my TIME is precious – sometimes more so than my money. One of the biggest keys to your success is systematizing and working the system! When you hire staff, you can either reinvent the wheel, or you can create one system and use it over and over again.

One of my business owner friends used to be a head hunter. A couple of years ago, I was so frustrated by the quality of applicants I was receiving in a position I was hiring. My friend asked to see both the job posting and the job description. After just about 30 seconds, she said that the problem was me and the job posting. She started to pick apart the job description and said that my ad was written to attract low quality leads.

So in just about 15 minutes, we were able to rewrite the job posting and job description. We didn't change the position. We only changed how the position sounded! This small change, and minimal time investment, brought me one of the best sets of candidates I've ever received in hiring. In Studio In a Box, we provide you with proven job postings, job descriptions, manuals, and training checklists.

When you are creating your job positing and job description, you want to list:
- What the primary job duties will be
- What the secondary job duties will be
- What educational requirements you have
- What experiential requirements you have
- What you are willing to pay for the position
- What time requirements the position holds (nights, weekends, full time, part time).

Use your job posting and job description once and identify what type of candidates you receive. And adjust accordingly.

When interviewing, do you have standard interview questions? I've said it once and I'll say it again, the more you systematize your business, the simpler and smoother it will run – with less time and energy from you! You can NOT ask about age, health, sexuality, marital status, or other family questions.

You do want to ask about their:
- Education
- Past Jobs
- Skills
- Technology used
- Sales History
- What they loved/hated about past jobs
- What they are looking for in your position
- Do they have the availability for the position?
- Do they have sales skills?
- References

When I am looking to hire, I make all applicants jump through some hoops. I ask them all to include a cover letter and I ask for certain things in their cover letters. I do this for a couple of reasons.

1. I can see how well they portray themselves in writing.
2. By putting in a few "hoops" or things to include, I can also identify if the potential staff person can follow directions.

As I've stated, my time is my most precious commodity. I need my staff to be able to take my instructions and implement them quickly, easily, and independently. If a potential staff person can't (or doesn't) follow instructions, then they have likely shown that they aren't the best fit for me before I ever need to speak to them!

I often post a position and ask potential applicants to include a resume, a cover letter with a paragraph about something they love to do in their free time, references. You would be amazed at how frequently they don't include a cover letter, never the less, the paragraph or references. If they couldn't follow instructions to GET the job, will they follow instructions once they have the job????

Do The Work:

Create a list of questions that you will use for interviews.

Creating a staff handbook

Your staff manual will cover all the things that you need to disclose to potential employee. This is a MAJOR piece of your new employee package. Your employee manual details many of the expectations you may have of your staff, and what they can expect from you. This is also a place that you want to include the things that are legally required by your state for your employees.

Practical Application

In California, there are specific laws about lunch breaks. One is that if someone works more than five hours, they are required to take a 30-minute unpaid lunch break. This was something that California started cracking down on over the past few years because employers were encouraging their staff to work through lunch.

In the studio, the morning shift starts at 8 am and ends at 12:50 pm. The shift is actually less than 5 hours. But if the staff arrived early or stayed late, it could quickly and easily cross that five-hour mark. So, we were required to update the employee manual to include the fact that if they were working over five hours in a shift that they were legally required to clock out and take a break. We needed to document that requirement! It was still a struggle even months and years later, requiring us to continually email the reminder of the requirement.

It was actually an unfortunate situation for the staff because if they were working for only five hours that day, they really didn't want to clock out and take a lunch break! But legally we are required to provide this and we are required to disclose this. We also have written in the employee manual, that is it THE STAFF'S responsibility to meet this obligation! This helps protect us in the event that they don't meet the requirement.

Your employee manual should include some (or all of) the following based on your company circumstances:
- Non-Discrimination Policy
- Drug Policy
- Sexual Harassment Policy
- Employment Laws
- Lunch Break/Staff break Requirements

- Overtime (if full time staff)
- Holidays and Holiday Pay
- Benefits Your Company Will Offer
- Dress Code (if you have one)
- Parking
- Personnel Records

Don't cut corners here! Employment disputes can arise at any time. In addition to lunch breaks, the classification of employees and the payment of overtime are also very important. It is recommended that you document all these policies, and that you have your staff sign for receipt of the handbook. We have our staff sign that they received the handbook when they first start with our company. We also include the handbook in our employee member portal. This ensures that they have access to our up to date versions at all times!

Staff Training Systems

As I mentioned in your job description and hiring tips, systems are one of the keys to your success. When I first opened, I had a staff training manual, but I had NO training checklists. It led to mistakes, confusion, and frustration. It also led to staff not doing their job and claiming ignorance! I quickly learned that I needed Training Checklists. Now, our staff does two days of training, and they have to initial that they were trained on each item on the training checklist.

I also created a number of training videos for my new staff. Once they are hired and sign their offer letter, they get access to an online portal that provides training videos to watch before they ever even come in for their first training session. This is my first opportunity to tell them about my business in my words! It also sets the expectations before they ever come in. If they can't be bothered to complete the "homework" before their first training, then they are demonstrating their work ethic and commitment to me and the company right away.

Do The Work:

Take the job description that you created and create a training checklist for potential staff.

The Importance of Sales Scripts

There are a couple of schools of thought on sales scripts. There are some that feel that scripts are imperative and there are some that thing that scripts are detrimental to the success of a business. I believe that for a new team member, scripts may be the difference between success and failure. However, I also believe that customer service can't fully be scripted. So, I give my team some leeway in their scripts.

However, your staff is a representation of your business! It is imperative that you hire well and train well. Most businesses today are customer service businesses in some way or another. Every interaction you have with a client has the ability to help your business grow or harm your business! In a world of lousy customer service, if your company excels in this regard, that in itself may make the company wildly successful!

It is important that you know what the responsibilities of your staff will be and that they are very clearly communicated to your staff. This is done through job descriptions, staff manuals, and sales scripts. Procedures and systems are put in place normally after something doesn't go right. Once a mistake is made – we learn, and create policies that are designed to work around them. A staff manual, and sales scripts will help systematize your client procedures and ensure that clients are getting the best experience possible.

Hiring Your First Staff:

When you are ready to hire your first staff person, you need to determine what type of person you want to hire. But I believe that there are a few different ways to look at how you want to hire.

First, there are two things that you want to consider:
1. What you can't do
2. What you don't want to do.

The first category is super simple – is there something that you feel needs to be done in the business that you just don't feel that you have the capabilities to do. For example, I have outsourced a number of technical tasks. These are things that I know how to do just enough to get myself in trouble. Imagine being

I could learn how to do many of these technical skills, but it would take a much longer period of time and would cause much more frustration than warranted. For example, I have been working with a program called Leadpages. It is simple and easy to use. But is isn't quite as customizable for what I need. So I found a similar (but more complex) program called Clickfunnels. I could definitely learn how to use Clickfunnels. But it would NOT be a good use of my time or energy! So, that is something that I have recently offloaded.

However, I would likely have a hard time offloading booking my travel. I like to compare the times, prices, hotels, amenities, etc. I don't want to pass that decision making power off to someone else! Something I have NOT offloaded that I should is managing the client emails! I have always prided myself on my personal touch, but unfortunately I often feel overwhelmed and stressed out by the sheer volume of email. If I instead passed the support email address off to my assistant, I'd save myself time, stress, and frustration. (Guess what I get rid of tomorrow.)

Examples of things you would offload because you don't know how to do them (or do them well):
- Website Creation
- Facebook Advertising
- Sales Funnel Creation
- Graphic Design
- Book Keeping/Accounting
- Creating Video and Audio Files

Examples of things you would offload because you don't WANT to do them:
- Returning client emails
- Booking travel
- Managing your social media
- Administration

Things an assistant could do for you:
- Website creation
- Facebook advertising
- Sales funnel creation
- Graphic design
- Bookkeeping/accounting
- Creating video and audio files

- Returning client emails
- Booking travel
- Managing your social media
- Administration
- Researching and writing blog posts
- Uploading blog posts
- Researching competitors
- Managing your calendar
- Ordering supplies
- Grocery Shopping
- Errands

When you are determining if you should do a task or not, a good question to ask is this – is it something you want to do, and if it is, is it a good use of your time? If a task would take you five hours, but take someone else less than an hour – pass it off and do something else! As a business owner, you often believe you HAVE to work 80 hour weeks and sacrifice your personal life and your health for your business.

As you consider what you will offload, I encourage you to remember this quote, "You can have it all, as long as you don't try to DO it all." Once I started passing off some of the tasks I had always held as my own, that was the moment I was finally able to start taking more vacation time and the business started to run more smoothly – without me!!

Staffing Options:

- Hire one executive or personal assistant to oversee "all" your needs. This person will need either a wide variety of knowledge or experience, or you will need to prepare yourself to train them in all the tasks you want them to do.

- Hire a number of part time assistants who specialize in certain tasks.

There are no definitive guidelines for what you'll pay for each of these roles. Typically, the more experience or skill you are requiring, the more you will need to pay.

On Site Staff vs Virtual Staff

This may be an unpopular topic as we start to talk about outsourcing overseas, but I want to talk you through the options.

First, I have run my business for over six years and had always hired on site staff. I required that my staff come to my place of business and we worked face to face. Unfortunately, with increasing needs and increasing wages, it has become harder and harder to find the right skills and qualifications at a reasonable cost. I have needed writing assistance, video editing, blog posts, web work, graphic design, social media management, sales funnel assistance, and more! I have spent THOUSANDS of dollars and hours of time training people who were not up to the tasks at hand. Every time a staff person does not work out, it can cost you immeasurable amounts of time and money!!!

In California, there are a number of regulations that are making on site staff undesirable. First, minimum wage will be increasing to $15 per hour over the next year. Unfortunately, we already have an issue getting some of our staff to create enough quality work to make their current wages profitable for us. But as we are required to hire more labor with no regard to their skills for a minimum of $15 per hour, it will make the labor force VERY expensive – and gives you NO protection to the quality of your workers. Also, in California, even a part time worker who only works five hours a week is now entitled to a minimum amount of paid time off. This makes it less desirable, and more expensive, to have staff.

Then my biggest challenge is often the quality of the work received. I walked into my business one day after I hadn't been in all morning and found that a number of the tasks I had left for my staff had not been completed. When I opened the internet browser, imagine my frustration when I found that instead of doing the work that was assigned, that my staff person had spent five hours on YouTube watching music videos! I was so mad! I immediately told my husband I'd be firing this staff person if you have to "babysit" your staff to get them to complete the tasks assigned, they probably aren't the right staff for you.

When you hire your staff, I encourage you to have written in all your offer letters, handbooks, and contracts that the first 90 days are an introductory period and that at the end of the 90 days, you will meet together to determine if the position is the right fit!

Before hiring your staff, it is imperative that you know exactly what qualifications you are looking for, exactly what you plan to have your assistant work on, and how you will train them. A past business coach once told me to Hire Slow and Fire Fast! At first, you never really understand that statement. But a disgruntled staff person has the potential to steal money, steal data, make your clients unhappy and more!

Team Builder

What's the role of this new position? Create a clear and detailed job description.

_____

_____

_____

How will success be measured? What is the specific RESULT I am paying for?

_____

_____

_____

How can I create a compensation plan that incentivizes the behavior I am looking for?

_____

_____

_____

What specific experience, education, and training am I looking for in this position?

_____

_____

_____

What personal values, personality traits, and character qualities are needed to be a fit for this position and our team?

_____

_____

_____

What do I need to pay this person to make it a win/win? (Think incentives as well as base)

_____

_____

_____

Interview Protocols to Save Yourself Time and Hassle:

Be VERY descriptive of the position when you are posting the ad.

- In the ad, give VERY specific instructions. I ask for a separate cover letter asking them to answer a question (use one below), as well as a resume and their references. If they are applying to be an instructor, I ask for a photo. These "hoops" tell me if someone can read and follow instructions before I ever meet them.
- Host a phone appointment first. In less than 10 minutes on the phone, you can often determine if someone is enough of a fit to warrant an interview.

- If you have a manager/personal assistant that really knows you well, have them interview all candidates first. This will save you time and energy, and will help you only meet with the candidates that may be a better fit.

SAMPLE Interview:

- Describe the position, qualifications needed, skills, etc.
- Ask them the basics:
- Please tell me about your technology skills.

On a scale of 1-10, please rate your proficiency in:
- PC/Mac?
- Microsoft Office Suite?
- Google Docs/Google Drive?
- Social Media – Facebook for business, Facebook Ads, Twitter, Instagram, Have you ever used these for business?
- Google Ads
- ITunes to download and update music, apps, etc
- Other software programs, etc.
- What are your biggest strengths?
- How are you with people? Sales?

Role Play with them and see how they do.
- Have them sell you a membership
- Have them handle a tough customer situation.

What additional training do you think you will need from us to do the job well?

- If we're sitting here a year from now celebrating what a great year it's been for you in this role, what did we achieve together?

- When have you been most satisfied in your life?

- If you got hired, loved everything about this job, and are paid the salary you asked for, what kind of offer from another company would you consider?

- Who is your role model, and why?

- What things do you not like to do?

- Tell me about a project or accomplishment that you consider to be the most significant in your career.

- We're constantly making things better, faster, smarter or less expensive. We leverage technology or improve processes. In other words, we strive to do more--with less. Tell me about a recent project or problem that you made better, faster, smarter, more efficient, or less expensive.

- Discuss a specific accomplishment you've achieved in a previous position that indicates you will thrive in this position.

- What are your Strengths/Weaknesses?

- What questions do you have for me?

CHAPTER 12:
Balancing the Bustle

Time spent with those you love isn't spent -
it's invested
Author Unknown

The final chapter of this book is all about the much sought after "balance." As a business owner, you will find that your life may never really be all your own again! Your business often becomes your baby, and you will do almost anything to help it grow. As a new business owner, you will likely strive to find a routine that allows you maximum productivity while still allowing you free time. Just remember WHY you decided to become a business owner. Did you do it for the money? Did you do it for freedom?

When you first launch a business, you will likely need to spend more than 40 hours a week in your business. However, after a few months/years in business, you will likely have more freedom than you ever did when you were employed by someone else. The night I met Mike I asked him what he did. He said, "I have the best and worst boss in the whole wide world – myself." You see, he verbalized the exact challenge of being an entrepreneur. We can likely always do more. We can probably work ourselves into the ground if we don't make a conscious decision to live differently!

Your friendships will change. Your friends who are employees will likely not be able to understand your new schedule and your new life. They may not understand those months where there may be no money, especially if they get a bi-weekly paycheck. They may not understand when you get an "urgent" business call from your biggest client in the middle of your Christmas Eve dinner.

You can absolutely have more time and freedom as a business owner; you just have to be more deliberate.

As I write this today, I just came off a year of my life that enjoyed more vacation time than ever before. I had over 100 vacation days this past year, not including weekends! I traveled. I spent time with family. Mike and I closed up our laptops in the middle of the day on Wednesdays when the weather was great, just because we could!

As a business owner, there will be times that you will have to sprint! If you are creating new products, rolling out new services or are short staffed, you may have to work MORE and harder! There are times, however, that you will instead be able to reap the fruits of your labor and just sit back and enjoy a bit! THAT is your new balance!

The best things in life aren't things...
Amy Mewborn

Maintaining Your Personal Health

I know, we're already determined that you could sometimes literally work 24 hours a day, 7 days a week. You're not doing yourself or anyone around you any favors. I always liken it to being on a plane. When the little yellow mask comes down, you're supposed to put it on yourself first, THEN your kids.

It is the same with your own personal health. If you are stressed, overweight, not working out, or eating poorly, you are not going to be in the best position for your business. Your own health and wellness is super important. The best way to have more time for yourself and your personal health is to identify what you can offload in your daily routine!

Here are a few ideas…
- Consider having someone clean your house.
- Get healthy food delivered.
- Schedule your own workouts.

Schedule down time and relaxation time – and honor those commitments to yourself. Your health is irreplaceable. You would hate to wake up one day and find that you don't have it any more, and you have to spend all that hard earned wealth to get back that long, devalued health!

Today I was talking to a fellow business owner. She was in the middle of a huge deadline, and she was complaining of pure exhaustion. Because of this deadline, she was trying to push through and just get to Monday when the project was due. The problem was that this was the "project du jour," and last week there was another project and next week would bring another project with a tight deadline.

A few years ago, I learned that I was a sprinter. I could work really hard for a short period of time, as long as I knew there was a break coming. For me, every time I am completely spent, I either need a vacation, or I need a day to just stay in bed and watch TV! After a bit of time off, I can come back to my desk refreshed and often full of new ideas. Once I hit burn out, though, you aren't going to get good or creative ideas (or solutions) from me!

I want to ask you… What do you like to do to relax?

_____

_____

_____

If you had three days off in a row, how would you spend them to recharge your mind and your body?

_____

_____

_____

Pull out a calendar and schedule at least ONE of these days every single week for the next quarter. Ideally, you will get up to 2-5 of these days at a time, but at first, just to book ONE SINGLE day COMPLETELY off! Leave your phone off or put a message on saying that you are OFF that day! I promise, it will do wonders for your physical and mental health – and your business!

Maintaining Family Time

Along with your own personal health, one of the questions I frequently get is, "How do you maintain family time? If I run a business, will I still be able to do things with my family?" I want to be very clear. If your goal is to work 24/7, you can do that. If your goal is to work 10 - 20 hours a week and you're willing to outsource a few more tasks, you can do that too. I spend about 5 hours a week in the studio. I spend a number of other hours creating content, designing choreography, creating marketing materials, meeting with staff, etc. My serious, in studio work time, however, is now less than 5 hours a week.

At the beginning of this book, I asked you to create some goals. This is a great time to revisit those goals.

- Do you want to take Fridays off with your family?
- Do you want to work from 9 am to 2 pm 4-5 days a week?

As the business owner, if you have enough staff, you are the architect of your schedule and your life. Create it, own it, and don't feel guilty! Mike and I live in San Diego. It is not uncommon to experience an 80-degree day in December on a Wednesday! We have found that one of our favorite things to do on these days is to play "hooky" and go have lunch at one of the beach front restaurants, complete with a margarita or sangria!

We know that for as hard as we work in our day to day, we have earned those days, and we don't feel bad when we take them. We have also learned that we often work till 11 pm. So, if we want to sleep in till 9am and sit over a cup of coffee and strategize before we start our business day, we do. We don't feel bad about it. We don't have kids, but we value our time together.

How to Do Only What Is Important

As a business owner, you will be BUSY! There NEVER seems to be enough time in the day. I swear that some days I could work all 24 hours and still not get "it" all done. So, I am always looking for ways to save myself time. Here is a great way to determine if you are using your time effectively.

Evaluate how you are actually spending your time. Some days, I work all day long but don't feel like I really get one thing done. As I mentioned, I once worked with a productivity expert to evaluate the efficiency of my week. What I found was that I was doing a lot of tasks that really weren't necessary, but I was also doing a lot of tasks that shouldn't have been mine.

As the business owner, you are the CEO of that business. You shouldn't be the one calling the software company about a technical glitch. You probably shouldn't be the one responding to the client emails either, and don't even get me started on how much time you are probably losing "playing" on social media.

So tomorrow, I want you to track how you are spending your day. I encourage you to set a timer for every two hours. At the time the timer goes off, write down how you just spent the last two hours. You will find that this task is very telling! You may think that you spend all day working, when really you just spent 40 minutes of the past two hours on Facebook or replying to emails that didn't really need your immediate attention.

To improve your work/life balance, I also encourage you to block a few hours each day when you put your phone on "do not disturb" so you are not receiving phone calls, texts, or social media notifications. By switching back and forth between your task at hand and the "interruptions," you are losing precious focus and productivity.

Practical Application

In finance, whenever I was on a deadline, I would place a message on my voice mail that stated that I was working on a very important client project and that I would be checking messages and returning phone calls between the hours of 11 and noon and again between 3 and 4. This allowed me to run calculations and make complicated financial comparisons without interruption, thus making me more productive AND reducing the number of mistakes!

How to Get More Done in Less Time

We already covered how you can take on fewer tasks. Now let's see if we can make what you do more time efficient! Automate and systematize ANYTHING that you can. Anything that you do more than once a month should have a system set up for it. For example, if you get a lot of similar client requests via email, there should be an email script that you can just copy and paste (or even set up as an auto responder). If you send a monthly newsletter, there should be a template. If you have bills that are paid each month, set them up on auto debit (from your credit card - NOT your bank account). Simplify and systematize anything that you can!

Also, batch your projects! I mentioned my productivity expert. What I didn't mention was all the energy that I was wasting by only doing half of my tasks and saving more for later or switching gears as the day went on. The energy that is required to send client emails is very different from the energy required for bill paying, which is very different from the energy required for teaching classes or clients. My Mondays are my studio client days, but after teaching 3-4 high energy classes, I am in NO shape to write emails, handle client service issues, etc. Those ALWAYS wait until Tuesday if they need me to handle them. I only pay bills twice a month, and I have asked my vendors to set me up on billing for the 1st and for the 16th; so that when I sit down to pay everyone it coincides with payroll, and I'm handling almost all the finances for the business over only two days in a month.

So, if you're a high-energy business owner (or aspiring to be a high-energy business owner), these three tips will save you tons of time and help you get MORE done - and still have more time for yourself!

My final piece of advice to you as a new business owner is to make yourself a priority. I have told you the basic framework that you need to launch a new business and run it like the CEO that you are, but your health is your number one asset! All work and no play makes most of us unhealthy, unhappy business owners! Schedule free time and HONOR IT! Don't let other people derail your health, wellness, and relational goals. Balance can't be achieved each and every day, but with a concerted effort, you can build a business AND a life that you are passionate about.

Good luck and best wishes in the next phase of your life! I wish you all the happiness and success you could ever imagine!

I work to live… Not live to work
Amy Mewborn

About the Author:

Amy Mewborn is a serial entrepreneur, CEO, author, and operations expert. She teaches women business owners how to use technology and systems to leverage their business growth and maximize profits through automation. A 20+ year business advisor in finance, marketing, and operations, Amy has worked with the business owners of large organizations such as Ford, Vinturi, and Chuck E. Cheese, as well as burgeoning entrepreneurs. Her focus is on improving and automating systems to increase revenue, decrease expenses, stabilize income, and gain control over their finances and life.

Amy is a Certified Financial Planner and holds a Series 7, Series 63, and Series 24 – national financial designations. She has helped women pick up the baton in their multi-million-dollar family business after the passing of the family CEO, as well as helping women launch a new business.

Amy is the founder and CEO of Fit in 60 Pilates and Barre, a premier barre brand that helps certify instructors and helps women launch successful barre studios around the world with the tools and systems of a franchise, without the fees and rules.

Amy also runs Amy Mewborn Consulting where she speaks, educates, and consults on using technology and systems to create and launch online courses. She specializes in working with women who may already have a business coaching or one on one service business. She then teaches them to take their intellectual property to create training programs and stop trading dollars for hours. She is passionate about helping women achieve financial and lifestyle independence! Amy's goal is to transform how women do business and help create over one million financially independent women entrepreneurs by 2025!

You can learn more about Amy and her programs at amymewborn.com

You can get free resources mentioned in this book at amymewborn.com/free

CPSIA information can be obtained
at www.ICGtesting.com
Printed in the USA
FSOW04n2212181216
28734FS